Talking to Siri™

Erica Sadun
Steven Sande

que®

800 East 96th Street,
Indianapolis, Indiana 46240 USA

Talking to Siri™
Learning the Language of Apple's Intelligent Assistant

ISBN-13: 978-0-7897-4973-4

ISBN-10: 0-7897-4973-4

Library of Congress Cataloging-in-Publication data is on file.

Printed in the United States of America

First Printing: March 2012

Trademarks

All terms mentioned in this book that are known to be trademarks or service marks have been appropriately capitalized. Que Publishing cannot attest to the accuracy of this information. Use of a term in this book should not be regarded as affecting the validity of any trademark or service mark.

Siri is a trademark of Apple, Inc.

Day-Timer is a registered trademark of ACCO Brands Corporation.

Warning and Disclaimer

Every effort has been made to make this book as complete and as accurate as possible, but no warranty or fitness is implied. The information provided is on an "as is" basis. The authors and the publisher shall have neither liability nor responsibility to any person or entity with respect to any loss or damages arising from the information contained in this book or from the use of programs accompanying it.

Talking to Siri is an independent publication and has not been authorized, sponsored, or otherwise approved by Apple, Inc.

Bulk Sales

Que Publishing offers excellent discounts on this book when ordered in quantity for bulk purchases or special sales. For more information, please contact

> **U.S. Corporate and Government Sales**
> **1-800-382-3419**
> **corpsales@pearsontechgroup.com**

For sales outside the United States, please contact

> **International Sales**
> **international@pearsoned.com**

Editor-in-Chief
Mark Taub

Senior Acquisitions Editor
Trina MacDonald

Managing Editor
Sandra Schroeder

Senior Project Editor
Tonya Simpson

Copy Editor
Keith Cline

Indexer
Tim Wright

Proofreader
Kathy Ruiz

Publishing Coordinator
Olivia Basegio

Book Designer
Anne Jones

Compositor
Bumpy Design

Contents at a Glance

Table of Contents

Preface

With Siri, your spoken wishes are your iPhone's command. Debuting on the iPhone 4S, the voice-operated Siri assistant uses natural-language processing to answer your questions, respond to your commands, and provide assistance as you need it. With Siri, you can set up meetings, call your mom, ask about your appointments, check your email, find your friends, and a lot more.

It's incredibly convenient. You'll find yourself using your iPhone in ways you never did before because Siri makes things so much simpler. "Wake me up at 8:30 a.m." "Tell my wife I'm on my way home." "Remind me to stop by the dry cleaners when I leave here." Siri offers virtual concierge services that simplify your life.

This short book introduces you to Siri. You learn how to access the voice assistant by using the Home button, and how to achieve the highest recognition rate as you talk. You discover which categories Siri responds to and find out how to make the most of each of these in your conversations. You also discover practical how-to guidance mixed with many examples to inspire as well as to instruct.

Tutorials show you how to set up Siri in your preferences and how to manage the interactive conversations you have with your voice assistant. You learn how to perform tasks by topic: checking the weather, doing math, or looking up information on the Web.

Ready to get started? Here are all the basics you need for talking to Siri, presented in a simple, easy-to follow handbook.

What's New in This Print Edition

This edition contains all the material originally published in the ebook version of *Talking to Siri* and adds several extra sections and errata fixes.

Who This Book Is For

This book is written for anyone who has purchased a Siri-enabled iOS device and wonders how to make the most of it. If you're looking for tips, tricks, and how-to guidance, you've come to the right place. This book offers friendly, easy-to-read tutorials that show you, with a wealth of examples, the ins and outs of Siri use in real life.

How This Book Is Organized

This book offers topic-by-topic coverage of basic Siri usage. Each chapter groups related tasks together, allowing you to jump directly to the material you're looking for. Here's a rundown of what you find in this book's chapters.

- **Chapter 1, "Getting Started with Siri":** This chapter introduces you to Siri basics. You read about setting up the service, launching it, and trying it out. You discover how to speak clearly and how recover from mistakes when Siri misunderstands you.

- **Chapter 2, "Asking Siri for Information":** Want to check the weather or stocks? Need to search the Web? This chapter introduces ways you can check information by conversing with Siri. You read about Siri integration with Wikipedia and Wolfram Alpha and learn how to ask questions that get you the best possible answers.

- **Chapter 3, "Using Siri to Stay in Touch":** This chapter shows you how you can use Siri queries to keep in touch with your friends, family, and business contacts. You read about searching for contacts, placing phone calls, texting, and sending email. You learn about how Siri relationships work and how you can let Siri know who your spouse, your child, or your parent is.

- **Chapter 4, "Talking to Your Day-Timer":** When you want to create appointments, take notes, or set reminders, Siri provides the perfect set of tools for organizing your life. Siri enables you to check your daily schedule, jot down important notes, and set short-term timers and alarms. This chapter introduces all the ways you can use Siri to help schedule and organize your life.

- **Chapter 5, "Going Shopping with Siri":** Whether you're searching for goods and services, trying to find your way to local businesses, or trying to figure out tax and tip after eating lunch, Siri has the tools you need. In this chapter, you read about using Siri to go shopping. You discover great ways to hunt down the items you need and surprisingly useful tips on having Siri remind you about them when you get close to the stores that carry them.

- **Chapter 6, "Pushing Limits with Siri":** The Siri universe continues to expand over time. Even now, with a little clever planning, you can blog and tweet using Siri text messaging and SMS-enabled services. This chapter shows you how you can push the Siri envelope. You read about having fun with Siri and all the clever ways you can tickle your personal assistant's funny bone.

- **Chapter 7, "Dictation":** Siri does a lot more than just answer queries. Its built-in dictation support means you can use its natural language-to-text support to speak to any application on your iPhone. This chapter discusses all the ins and outs of Siri dictation, providing tips and hints about getting the most accurate responses, and shows how you can produce exactly the text you're looking to create (punctuation and all).

Contacting the Authors

If you have any comments or questions about this book, please visit http://sanddunetech.com/contact-us/. We're happy to listen to your feedback. Follow us on Twitter (@sanddunebooks) and http://talking2siri.com to keep up with our new ebooks.

About the Authors

Erica Sadun writes lots of books and she blogs at TUAW. When not writing, she's a full-time parent of geeks who are brushing up on their world-domination skills. According to her academic dosimeter, she has acquired more education than any self-respecting person might consider wise. She enjoys deep-diving into technology.

Steve Sande also writes way too much. He's the hardware editor at TUAW, and recently logged more than one million words written for the blog in just over 3 years. He's written a number of books for Take Control Books and Apress, is married to a rocket scientist, and spends his days being bossed by a cat.

Acknowledgments

We want to thank Megan Lavey-Heaton for her help on the cover for this book and to Mike Rose for his help with edits. Thanks, too, to everyone at TUAW for all their support and to all the readers and friends who helped with suggestions and feedback. None of this would have been possible without the vision and leadership of Apple's late founder and CEO, Steve Jobs. Thank you, Mr. Jobs.

We Want to Hear from You!

As the reader of this book, *you* are our most important critic and commentator. We value your opinion and want to know what we're doing right, what we could do better, what areas you'd like to see us publish in, and any other words of wisdom you're willing to pass our way.

As an editor-in-chief for Que Publishing, I welcome your comments. You can email or write me directly to let me know what you did or didn't like about this book—as well as what we can do to make our books better.

Please note that I cannot help you with technical problems related to the topic of this book. We do have a User Services group, however, where I will forward specific technical questions related to the book.

When you write, please be sure to include this book's title and author as well as your name, email address, and phone number. I will carefully review your comments and share them with the author and editors who worked on the book.

Email: feedback@quepublishing.com

Mail: Mark Taub
           Editor-in-Chief
           Que Publishing
           800 East 96th Street
           Indianapolis, IN 46240 USA

Reader Services

Visit our website and register this book at informit.com/register for convenient access to any updates, downloads, or errata that might be available for this book.

Getting Started with Siri

Perhaps the most widely known feature on the iPhone 4S is Siri. On the iPhone 4S, Siri replaces the dance of your fingers on the glass screen of the device with a conversation. Siri understands your voice, places what you say in context to the apps that it works with, and even responds with a question if it doesn't understand. For the first time outside of science fiction, we have a way to interface in natural language with a computer.

In this chapter, you learn how to get started with Siri: how to enable it, launch the service, and try it out. You read about how to speak (slowly and clearly), how to recover from mistakes, and how to access the service in a variety of ways. By the time you finish reading this chapter, you'll feel at ease talking to (instead of at) your iPhone 4S.

Enabling Siri

To ensure that the Siri service has been enabled, navigate to
Settings, General, Siri. Here you find a page of options that let you
control how Siri works. Figure 1-1 shows these options.

Figure 1-1
From the Siri Settings pane, you can choose a primary language, set when you want the service to
speak to you, and enable or disable the Raise to Speak option.

Switch the primary Siri toggle to ON to activate the service. When
the service is disabled (OFF), the built-in iOS VoiceControl feature
still enables you to place hands-free calls and request music. Siri is
a lot more powerful than VoiceControl, and offers a wider range of
voice-directed actions.

Disabling Siri also removes your information from Apple servers. If you want to reenable Siri later, it might take time to reestablish your personal information and profile.

The other options you find on this settings page include the following:

- **Language:** Select the language and region you want Siri to use for interpreting your interaction. In its initial release, Siri supported only English (US, UK, and Australia), French, and German. The set of supported languages and regions should grow over time as Siri is deployed throughout the world.

- **Voice Feedback:** Decide whether you want Siri to respond to you with voice as well as text responses. You can choose to always enable this feature or to support it only for hands-free operation (that is, when used with a headset of some sort). Keep in mind that Siri uses a separate volume control system from your main iPhone. If you enable voice feedback and forget to lower the Siri volume, you could encounter embarrassing situations in meetings by activating the service by accident.

- **My Info:** This sets the default contact for your identity. It's how Siri knows where "home" is, what your name is, and so forth. It also allows Siri to associate relationships with your contact, such as "my wife" or "my mother" or "my son." Make sure that it points to the right contact so that when Siri tries to help you, it's working with the right person.

- **Raise to Speak:** When enabled, Siri activates using the iPhone proximity sensor. This is the onboard sensor that tells if your face is near the iPhone screen. You can start a Siri session simply by raising the iPhone to your ear. You generally want to leave this option enabled because it offers the easiest way to activate Siri from your handset.

NOTE

Muting your iPhone and lowering the speaker volume to zero does not affect Siri chimes directly, for both dictation and voice assistance. If you hold the Home key for too long or if your finger brushes across the microphone in the keyboard, you could trigger a Siri-based beep. This can be quite embarrassing in boardroom or classroom situations. That's because Siri has its own volume control, which you access only when the assistant is shown onscreen.

Summon Siri, and then adjust the volume control down once the purple microphone is onscreen. Siri will be silenced, ensuring your Siri-enabled phone stays quiet even when you accidentally open the assistant screen. This doesn't affect the chime Siri plays (just to you) when you hold the phone up to your ear.

Universal Access

Siri works with VoiceOver, the screen reader built in to iOS. VoiceOver offers a way that visually impaired users can "listen" to their *graphical user interface* (GUI). VoiceOver converts an application's visual presentation into an audio description.

VoiceOver can speak any text displayed on your iPhone screen, including Siri responses. VoiceOver speech can also interpret certain graphical elements presented by Siri into speech. These include weather forecasts, emails, answers from Wolfram Alpha, and so forth.

You enable VoiceOver in Settings, General, Accessibility, VoiceOver. Make sure to set the Triple-Click Home option to ON; doing so allows you to enable and disable VoiceOver with a simple shortcut.

When using VoiceOver, you use the iPhone GUI with your fingers and ears rather than with your eyes. An entire language of touches is used with VoiceOver, entailing an associated learning curve. Consult documentation on Apple's website for details about using VoiceOver features both in general and with Siri.

Privacy

Apple collects data on your Siri usage. Information sent to Apple includes your contacts in the address book, your name and contact information, songs and playlists from your media library, audio recordings of you speaking, transcripts of what you have said, and *operating system* (OS) information/performance statistics. If you use Siri, a lot of your personal information is going to Apple.

What's more, this information may be shared with Apple's partners for dictation-related services, but will not be shared with other third parties. You cannot opt out of data collection, but you can opt out of Siri entirely by not using the feature and disabling it in Settings.

For more about Siri privacy issues, tap the About Siri and Privacy link in the Siri Settings pane (refer to Figure 1-1).

Launching Siri

Siri lets you use your voice instead of your fingers to send messages, schedule meetings, choose music, and more. You use Siri conversationally. You talk to your iPhone and your iPhone talks right back to you.

You can access Siri in several ways:

- Press and hold the Home button for a couple of seconds.
- Raise your iPhone to your ear.

- Engage it from your wired (iPhone earbud-style) or wireless (Bluetooth) headset by squeezing or pressing the control button. Siri also works with many car kits.

A chime tells you that Siri is listening and ready to follow your commands. Make sure that Siri is enabled and that you've got a good Internet connection. If so, you are ready to take off and start exploring this innovative voice-driven service.

 NOTE

Siri's recognition technology was created by an independent start-up founded by the Stanford Research Institute's Artificial Intelligence Center in 2007 (hence the name). The Siri company was acquired by Apple in 2010, and first debuted in iOS 5 on the iPhone 4S.

 NOTE

This book refers to Siri as it, not as him or her. This is because Siri has many voices, which are tied to localizations. These voices vary in gender based on the region in use. For example, in the United States, the default Siri voice is female, and in the United Kingdom, male.

Saying Hello to Siri

Siri uses several chimes. These let you know when it's listening to you. A higher chime starts a session, and a lower one finishes it. To hear this, raise your phone to your ear, and then place it back down on a table. The high chirps mean Siri is listening; the low chirps mean it is done listening.

Try the following: raise the phone to your ear, wait for the preliminary chirps, say "Hello," and then pause. Siri uses pause detection to know when you've stopped speaking. Again, you hear the second set of chirps, but this time you hear them without moving the phone away from your ear.

If you have a good Internet connection—a requirement of working with Siri—you'll hear it respond to you. Siri responds "Hi" or "Hello," perhaps adding your name (see Figure 1-2, top). As you talk, Siri creates a scrolling list of responses, so you can review the conversation to date. By default, Siri automatically scrolls up to the most recent response, so you might want to pull down on the list to see what has gone before.

Siri also provides suggestions on what to say. Just say "Help me" or "What can you do?" Siri displays a list of categories (such as Phone, Music, Messages, Calendar) along with a sample phrase for each topic. Tap on any category (Figure 1-2, top) to see a more complete list of sample phrases for that category (Figure 1-2, bottom left).

Siri responds to touch interaction as well as to raising your phone to your ear. To initiate a Siri session, press and hold the Home button for about 1 to 2 seconds. Siri plays its initial chime and automatically starts listening.

Canceling Siri

If you ever need to stop whatever Siri is doing, just say, "Cancel," and then tap the microphone button or press the Home button.

Because Siri remembers your ongoing thread of conversation, you might need to reset your current conversation at times. Say "Start over" or "Restart" to begin a fresh new dialog. Siri responds with a response such as "Okay, Erica, what's next?" or "What can I help you with?"

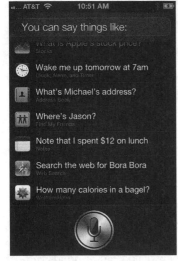

Figure 1-2
Saying hello to Siri (top), asking Siri for help (bottom left), viewing sample phrases (bottom right).

Quitting Siri

Leave Siri mode by pressing the Home button. In the initial Siri rollout, it's clear that Apple meant to support "Goodbye" as an alternative way to leave Siri. If you say "Quit," Siri responds, "Did I say something wrong? If you really want me to go away, at least say 'goodbye.'" and "Quit? Did you mean 'goodbye'?" For now, the Home button remains the best way to return to normal iOS touch-based operations.

Hopefully, Apple will fully implement a spoken leave-by-command feature in future firmware updates.

Siri Listens

As Siri listens, look at the microphone in the center of the Siri button at the bottom of the screen (refer to Figure 1-2, bottom right). This microphone acts as a level meter for your spoken input. It provides you with volume feedback as you speak and lets you know that Siri is in listening mode. If you do not respond after a few seconds, Siri stops listening and plays the end-of-listening chime.

To finish speaking, either pause and wait for Siri or you tap the Siri button. After listening, Siri enters thinking mode. During this time, a purple glow circles around the button, letting you know that Siri is contacting Apple's data centers for speech interpretation and processing. Siri works with both 3G and Wi-Fi Internet connections.

If Siri is able to process your statement, it tries to interpret it and provide some kind of response for you. If Siri cannot call home to its Apple data processing center, it informs you about the situation, saying something like, "I'm sorry, I'm having difficulty accessing the network." Try moving to a location with a better Internet signal or try again later.

NOTE

> Siri works with many audio accessories, including Apple's
> iPhone earbuds (the ones with the built-in microphone and
> squeeze control), Bluetooth headsets, and car hands-free kits.

Siri Responds

Siri responds to both direct commands and to random statements. If what you said cannot be interpreted as a request, Siri
offers to search the Web for your statement. For example, Figure
1-3 (left) shows how Siri responds to the word *platypuses*. If you
choose to Search the Web, Siri uses your word or phrase for a
web search using your default engine. Set your default search
engine in Settings, Safari, Search Engine, and choose from Google,
Yahoo!, and Bing.

Figure 1-3
Siri offers web searches for any words/phrases it doesn't immediately recognize (left). Tap your
speech bubble to edit it directly or redictate your statement (right).

NOTE

Siri learns your accent and voice characteristics over time. As long as you keep Siri enabled in your iPhone settings, your Siri account remains on Apple's servers and your recognition rates improve over time. Siri uses voice-recognition algorithms to categorize your voice into its database of regional dialects and accents. This database continues to evolve, and will continue to improve as Siri collects more data and evaluates its interpretation successes. Siri also uses information from your iPhone. Data from your contacts, music library, calendar, and reminders helps fuel its recognition vocabulary.

To reset your Siri information, switch Siri OFF and then back ON in Settings, General, Siri. This disposes of all personalized settings Siri has collected from you over time (not including any general metrics it studies and adds to its primary database) and returns Siri to a fresh install, ready to learn your quirks again.

Correcting Siri

Siri always gives you a second chance. To fix what you said or correct Siri's interpretation of your speech, just tap the speech bubble that represents what you said (Figure 1-3, right). When you do, the bubble turns white and the system keyboard appears. At this point, you can type directly into the bubble. You can edit your request directly or tap the microphone button on the keyboard to redictate your request. Tap Done to finish.

Sometimes Siri's dictation processor adds a blue line under a word in the text you have spoken. When you tap that word, iOS presents alternative interpretations of your speech. Select the correction you want to use or edit, or dictate a replacement.

You can also speak to correct text messages or mail contents that you have composed. The following examples let Siri know that you're not satisfied with what you've said. Notice how you can change the contents completely, add new material, and so forth:

- Change it to: Let's meet at 3:00 p.m.
- Add: Can't wait exclamation point. (You can use "add" to extend items, even if Siri doesn't mention it explicitly as an option.)
- No, send it to Megs.
- No. (This keeps the message without sending it.)
- Cancel.

Before you send a text message on its way, have Siri read it back to you. Say "Read it to me" or "Read it back to me." Like the "add" feature, Siri does not tell you about this option. When you are satisfied with your text or email message, say something like "Yes, send it" to send it off.

Enhancing Your Speech Recognition

Siri responds to commands by creating appointments, setting timers, placing phone calls, and more. To see this in action, try creating a new note. Say, "Note that I spent $15 on lunch." Speak steadily, but do not draaaaag ooooooout what you're saying. Siri should reply, "Noted" or "Got it!" or something like that (see Figure 1-4, left).

When talking to Siri, remain conversational. Try to speak with normal tones and inflections, although you'll want to slow down slightly. Enunciate a bit more than you're used to, like a somewhat pedantic teacher. The key to Siri is holding on to your standard speech patterns while emphasizing any words that help Siri understand you better.

 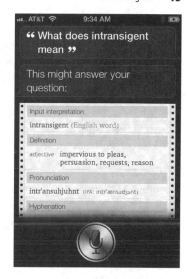

Figure 1-4
Siri can take notes but cannot delete them (left). Use slow, careful speech to increase Siri's recognition rate, like in this word-definition request (right).

Don't be afraid to ask questions (where your voice rises at the end), make statements (where your voice goes down), or otherwise speak sentences as you normally do, including emphasizing words inside sentences (for example, "What does *intransigent* mean?"). Do not try to be robotic or lose normal sentence inflections. Your recognition rate will plummet if you do.

This particular query ("What does intransigent mean?") should load up a definition, as shown in Figure 1-4 (right). It's actually a little hard to speak this request coherently and in a way that Siri understands, and so makes a good exercise to test out your speaking skills.

Clarity

Siri likes when you speak slowly and clearly, and when you e-nun-ci-ate your words, especially word-ending consonants. This helps Siri differentiate between, for example, *me* and *mean*. This is an important distinction when defining words, as in this example with *intransigent*, because asking Siri "What does *intransigent* me?" won't load the dictionary definition you're looking for, but "What does *intransigent* mean?" does.

Don't be afraid to add a little extra pause between words so that Siri can tell the difference between Mike Rose and micros, or Mike Rose's phone and microphone.

If you add too long a pause, Siri stops listening, but that does not happen accidentally. A good deal of usable range exists between your normal speaking speed and the extreme where Siri thinks you're not talking any more. Explore that range and test out longer pauses to see how you can improve your recognition.

Fumbles

Everybody fumbles words sometimes. If you find yourself stumbling over a tongue-twister, either edit your current entry or cancel it entirely. Tap the microphone twice. The first tap ends your entry. The second cancels the current processing. The rotating purple "thinking" animation stops, and the microphone button returns to its quiescent state, letting you know that Siri is ready and waiting for your next command.

Never worry about starting your request over. Siri doesn't care, and you can save a lot of time that would otherwise be wasted editing or waiting on interpretations of flubbed speech that are bound to go wrong.

Viewing Items You Create

Figure 1-4 (left) showed how you might create a note using Siri. Tap on any Siri note item to view it in the Notes application. That is also where you need to go if you want to delete the note you just created. Siri does not allow you to delete notes directly. That's because, as an assistant, Siri is directed toward creating new requests (notes, appointments, phone calls, dictation, weather checks) and not toward editing or application control in general. Siri is not a full voice interface.

The philosophy behind Siri is to offer a tool that enables you to accomplish simple creation and checking tasks hands free, while on the go. But that's where Siri's capabilities end. Don't expect to navigate through menus, search for information within documents, or otherwise treat Siri as a full artificially intelligent user interface. Knowing what Siri can and cannot do will help limit your expectations while using this tool.

This tapping trick works with most Siri items, not just notes; tap on contacts to view them in the Contacts app, or text messages in Messages, and so on. Siri often gives you items to choose from and actions to perform, as well; tap on these choices to select a contact or perform web searches, or you can instruct Siri by voice, specifying how you want to proceed.

Multilingual Siri

Unfortunately, the Siri voice assistant cannot directly switch languages (see Figure 1-5). The only way to change from English to French, for example, is to hop out, edit your preferences, and hop back in (Settings, General, International, Voice Control, Siri).

Figure 1-5
Siri cannot switch languages on-the-fly.

A workaround for multilanguage dictation exists, however. The Settings, General, International, Keyboards preferences allow you to add keyboards, enabling the globe button; when it is enabled, you can toggle directly between keyboard languages. You'll find it between the number toggle (123) and the microphone dictation button on the keyboard when you've enabled more than one language on your device.

A simple tap takes you to the next language setting, including dictation. By tapping, you move from French to English and back as you dictate into any text-entry element on your iPhone.

Hopefully, Siri will support "Speak to me in [some language]" requests in a future update.

NOTE

Siri recognizes each language using specific dialects and accents. Native speakers will experience higher recognition accuracy.

 NOTE

Apple announced it will ship support for Japanese, Chinese, Korean, Italian, and Spanish in 2012.

Living with Siri Limitations

At the time of its launch, Apple made clear that Siri was a beta product—flaws and all. Even when it is mature, you'll still expect that the voice-interpretation system will be subject to mistakes. After all, humans misunderstand things all the time. With the best of intentions and the best of interpretations, Siri will never be able to provide 100% accuracy. Consider Figure 1-6. It shows perfectly how Siri might always be limited.

Figure 1-6
What Erica meant (above) and what Siri interpreted (below).

Erica wanted Siri to play Pachelbel Canon in D. Instead, Siri offered to search for local Taco Bells. The similarity in phonemes, the basic units of speech used to construct the two phrases *Pachelbel* and *Taco Bell* meant that Siri's algorithms had to pick a more likely interpretation. It went with the latter, even though she intended the former.

This kind of incorrect response is, luckily, uncommon enough that it doesn't interfere with your normal day-to-day use of Siri.

Summary

Siri provides a new and natural way to interact with a computer, understanding your voice and a number of commands, and then doing your bidding and responding through speech or a visual answer on the iPhone screen. In this chapter, you gained an understanding of how to work with Siri. Some key points to take away from this discussion are as follows:

- Think carefully about the information you are sending to Apple when you agree to enable Siri. That's a lot of personal information you are trusting Apple with.

- If you don't know what to say, ask Siri to "Help me." It is always happy to provide a list of categories and sample phrases.

- You access Siri by pressing and holding the Home button, raising your iPhone to your ear, or squeezing or pressing the control button on a wired or wireless headset.

- Remember that Siri is more about creating items than editing them. Build new appointments, create new notes, write emails, but don't expect to cancel, delete, undo, or modify those items using the Siri interface.

- Talk slowly and clearly to Siri. Siri works best when you enunciate deliberately.

- Siri talk bubbles typically lead to more actions, allowing you to jump into associated apps like the Notes app for notes or the Contacts apps for addresses. You can tap both on your own talk bubbles and the ones Siri speaks to you.

- Don't be afraid of making mistakes with Siri. You can always reset your conversation or edit your speech bubble. Siri is designed to assist you, not to put obstacles in your way. Siri lets you add new text, edit the text you've already spoken, or redo your dictation from scratch. Use these tools to achieve the highest possible recognition rate.

- Siri uses a separate audio volume system. So if you're at a movie or a conference, make sure to mute your system audio *and* lower Siri's volume control. To do that, invoke Siri and use the volume toggles on the side of the phone to lower the Siri sound level.

- Siri simplifies your life. Whether it's setting alarms ("Wake me at 7.15"), finding a friend ("Where Is Barbara Sande?"), or updating your family ("Message my husband I'm on the way"), Siri is there to help you become more productive with less work. The more you learn about using Siri, the simpler these tasks become over time. For so many of these items, the issue isn't whether Siri can handle those tasks; it's whether you know that they're there to use them. If this book helps you add a few essential ideas into your day-to-day Siri use, then we've proudly done our jobs.

Asking Siri for Information

Siri exists to serve you. It wants nothing more than to give you information about just about anything in the universe. Siri provides you with answers to questions about everything from the weather to stock prices through integration with the apps that come with your iPhone 4S.

Questions outside the realm of the built-in apps on the iPhone are no problem for Siri. It knows how to work with Wikipedia and Wolfram Alpha, and searches the Web for the best possible answers to whatever you ask. In this chapter, you learn how to phrase your conversation with Siri in such a way to maximize the probability of getting an accurate and detailed answer.

Weather

Siri keeps on top of the weather forecast for you. When you ask, "Will it rain tonight?" (Figure 2-1) or "What is the temperature?" Siri offers immediate feedback. Asking "What's the weather for this week?" provides the full weekly forecast. As a rule, Siri replies with simple answers. If extensive charts are involved, you are prompted to look at the phone rather than just listening.

Figure 2-1
Siri can check the weather for you.

Other Queries

In addition to the current weather conditions, Siri provides sunrise and sunset times (for the current day only), the phase of the moon (although Siri sometimes balks depending on whether the information is available for the moon phase), and you can even ask "When will Jupiter (or Mars or Venus or the Moon or so on) rise?" to query about planets.

Siri has no access to past weather information and cannot check things like sunrise/sunset times for the future. So you cannot ask, "When will the sun rise tomorrow?" If you do, Siri reports only today's time.

Locations

If you switch between locations, make sure you let Siri know. When you ask about the high today in London and then ask about the local wind speed, Siri defaults to the London wind speed, not the local one, unless local for you *is* London. So go ahead and say "What's the wind speed here?" rather than "What's the wind speed?" to make sure you correct for the previous query.

Siri always tries to retain context for your conversations, to make it easier for you to add brief questions without having to keep stating who, where, and when, but these assumptions work against you if you don't specify "here" or "now" when changing the topic.

The best questions to ask in hands-free mode are ones that evaluate the weather, using specific quantities (how cold is it, how warm is it, what is the wind chill) or that specify will it rain/be cold/be hot, and so on. Figure 2-2 shows this kind of question in action. Siri replies with a useful narrated response.

 NOTE

When temperatures drop fast, Siri may add a "Brr" to your weather report. Amusingly, Siri originally said "Bee Arr Arr" when making this comment. Someone at Apple took note and taught Siri to pronounce the word as "Berrrr."

Figure 2-2
Siri can answer questions that evaluate the weather.

Siri offers a wide vocabulary of weather-related conversation. You can ask about forecasts using many approaches. Here are some things you can say to Siri about the weather.

- What's the weather for today?/What's the weather for tomorrow?
- What's the weather in London?
- Should I take an umbrella tomorrow?
- Should I wear a coat tonight?/Can I wear a bikini?
- Is it raining in Paris?

- How hot is it today?/How cold is it?
- What is the wind speed?/What is the wind speed in London right now?
- What is the humidity?/What is the wind chill?
- Will it rain in Cupertino this week?
- Will there be a storm here?
- Check next week's forecast for Burlington.
- What's the forecast for this evening?
- Will it snow this week in Denver?
- How's the weather in Tampa right now?
- How hot will it be in Palm Springs this weekend?
- What's the high for Anchorage on Thursday?
- What's the temperature outside?
- How windy is it out there?
- Is it nighttime in Paris?/When is sunrise in Paris?

Web Search

With Siri, you have the entire Web not just at your fingertips but also at the tip of your tongue. With spoken phrases, you can ask Siri to search the Web and show you the information it finds.

Siri uses several key phrases to hunt for information on the Web. You can tell it, "Search the Web," "Search the Web for [topic]," or "I want to see websites about…," among other web-oriented queries. Here are examples of web search requests you might ask Siri to perform:

- Search the Web for Bora Bora.
- Search for vegetarian pasta recipes.

- Search the Web for best cable plans.
- Search for news about the World Cup.
- I want to see websites about ostriches.
- Show me websites about baseball.

What's more, any of iOS's three major search engines are usable when you make your queries; so Google, Yahoo!, and Bing are all valid sources for information. For example, you might "Yahoo Redskins scores," "Google Knitting," or "Bing Parry Grip" (see Figure 2-3).

Figure 2-3
You can use search engine names as request verbs with Siri.

Searching for Pictures

If you're looking specifically for pictures, there's a shortcut for that, too. Say, "I want to see pictures of [topic]." For example, you might request, "I want to see pictures of kittens" (see Figure 2-4).

Figure 2-4
Siri understands requests that start with "I want to see…" and will start a meaningful web search for you.

Searching in Wikipedia

Siri offers full Wikipedia support. All you have to do is ask your question the right way. Here are some ways to ask for information from the vast treasure hoard of Wikipedia. Knowing that you have to specify Wikipedia as part of your statement is the majority of the battle:

- Search Wikipedia for Abraham Lincoln.
- Look up snowballs in Wikipedia.
- Search for eagles in Wikipedia.

The Search the Web Option

Whenever Siri cannot immediately respond to your request, it offers a web search on the topic you requested. For example, if you say "bluebirds," Siri says, "I don't know what you mean by your topic." It offers a Search the Web button, which you can tap. This opens Safari and searches for the phrase you spoke, using your current default search engine.

Making the Most of Your Search

TUAW reader Harris Rydal sent me a bunch of terrific ways to use Siri's built-in search features without having to do a lot of typing. These are, in my opinion, exceptionally useful ways of taking advantage of Siri-to-Safari tasking:

- **Sports scores:** Look up the current score for in-progress games and find the team record, last game score, and the upcoming game. Say "Yahoo [team name] score." Rydal points out the word *Yahoo* is included here because mobile Yahoo! formats the results better than Google.

- **Flight times:** Say "Search the Web for flights from [city/airport] to [city/airport]." In Google, this brings up a list of flight times that day and the associated airline. Unfortunately, you cannot use this for future flights at this time. You can say, "Search the Web for flights on December 18 from Denver to Charlotte," but you will just load a general web search for Denver/Charlotte flights.

- **Movie times (and ticket purchasing):** Say "[Movie name] show times [optional ZIP code]" or "Search for show times [ZIP code]." Rydal points out that if you've set Google in Safari to use your current location, you don't even need to specify a ZIP code. Google's Fandango integration enables you to click the show time and hop over to the ticket-purchasing page.

Checking Stocks

For those of us who have money in the stock market either through personal choice or a 401(K) plan that was foisted on us at work, it's occasionally interesting to see how bad our investments are doing by checking on stock prices. Because a stock ticker is part of the iOS 5 notification center and a Stocks app has been part of the iPhone since 2007, it's not surprising that Apple chose to have Siri be your personal investment assistant (see Figure 2-5).

Figure 2-5
Siri supplies up-to-the-minute information about the markets and individual stocks, but won't tell you what to buy or sell.

Not only does Siri give you an overall snapshot of the market averages, but it also supplies details about individual stocks. Here's an overview of some of the phrases that Siri understands. Just ask about the company name and Siri looks up the stock details.

- How is Proctor and Gamble doing?
- What's Coca Cola trading at?
- What's Apple's stock price?
- What is Apple's PE ratio?
- What did Yahoo! close at today?
- How is the Nikkei doing?
- How are the markets doing?
- What is the Dow at?
- What did Apple close at?
- What was Apple's high this year?

If you say, "Buy 500 shares of Apple," Siri looks up the stock, but it will not place an order. That's because Siri cannot actually offer stock services, or even advice. Apple definitely does not want Siri to be your stock advisor. I gave it a try, as you can see in Figure 2-6. Here are some examples of Siri queries that cause the assistant to complain. None of these produce the results you're looking for:

- Should I buy Apple?
- Siri, what are the 10 best picks on the New York Stock Exchange?
- Please pick me a good stock.

Figure 2-6
"What would I do? I'd shut it down and give the money back to the shareholders." (Michael Dell in 1997, answering a question about what could be done to fix the then-ailing Apple Computer, Inc.)

Using Wolfram Alpha

Wolfram Alpha is, according to Wikipedia, "an online service that answers factual queries directly by computing the answer from structured data, rather than providing a list of documents or web pages that might contain the answer as a search engine might."

Between Wikipedia and Wolfram Alpha, Apple has done an amazing job in opening up Siri searches to first-class information sources. Unlike Wikipedia queries, which open in the Safari browser, Wolfram Alpha answers are presented directly in the Siri interface. That makes it easy for you to keep going with a conversation, without having to hop into and out of Siri mode on your iPhone (see Figure 2-7).

Figure 2-7
Use Wolfram Alpha queries to check definitions, look up information, calculate, and more.

When Siri recognizes a question that might be best answered or analyzed by Wolfram Alpha, it passes along your data and then displays whatever Wolfram Alpha returns. Siri uses this special view to present those results. They aren't verbally announced to you. Some of the questions you can get answers to seem incredible.

Querying Wolfram

Wolfram knows about quite a lot. The most reliable way to query Wolfram is to prefix your question with "Wolfram," "Ask Wolfram," or "What is." The "Wolfram" clue isn't strictly necessary, as you'll see in the following sample statements. Each of these statements is interpreted by Siri and then passed to Wolfram Alpha without explicitly using the word *Wolfram* at all.

- How many calories in a bagel?
- What is an 18% tip on $86.74 for four people?
- What's Morse code for horse feathers?
- Who's buried in Grant's tomb?
- How long do dogs live?
- What is the Gossamer Condor?
- What are the first 23 digits of *e*?
- How many dollars is ¥50,000?
- What was best picture in 1949?
- How many days until Easter?
- How many days between September 22, 1957 and today?
- How far away is Neptune?
- When is the next solar eclipse?
- What is the orbital period of Pluto?
- Show me the constellation of Ursa Major.
- What's the population of Montenegro?
- How high is Mt. Kilimanjaro?
- How deep is the Pacific Ocean?
- What's the price of diesel in Dubuque, Iowa?

- What's the price of lettuce in New York City?
- What's the integral of the cosine of *x*? (Siri and Wolfram Alpha seem to have problems with the sine function, confusing it with the word *sign*.)
- Graph $y = 9x^2 + 2$ ("Graph *y* equals 9 x-squared plus 2")
- What's the derivative of $3x^3 + 2x$? ("What's the derivative of 3 x-cubed plus 2 x?")
- What's the boiling point of iron?
- What's the scientific name of a mountain lion?
- What's the atomic weight of lead?

Yes, Siri answers all these questions with the help of Wolfram Alpha and presents the results directly to you.

The depth of knowledge that Wolfram Alpha has is staggering. With Siri translating your questions into a format that Wolfram Alpha can understand, you have access to an incredible amount of information. Neither tool is perfect, and sometimes the way that Siri or Wolfram Alpha interprets your questions is amusing (to say the least), but they provide a huge amount of information and trivia.

Wolfram Mode

At times, Siri goes into what we call Wolfram mode. To see this for yourself, say "Ask Wolfram" and then pause. From that point, Siri tries to get you to ask a question that it can look up for you on that website.

Whenever this happens, tell Siri "Never mind." At least at the time this book was being written, the Wolfram mode was highly unstable and didn't seem to process the queries properly. Hopefully, Apple will address this bug in short order.

The Wolfram Saving Throw

Try saying "88 miles per hour" to Siri on your iPhone. Siri does not know an answer, but offers to perform a web search for you. In this case, you might want to use what we call the Wolfram saving throw, which allows Wolfram to act as a superhero. Tap the microphone and say the magic phrase, "Ask Wolfram."

Suddenly, bingo! Without any further work, Siri redirects your query to Wolfram Alpha—and saves the day. Figure 2-8 shows this maneuver in action.

Figure 2-8
The Wolfram saving throw converts a misunderstood phrase into a valid Wolfram Alpha search.

Wolfram Alpha Trick Lets You Know What Is Flying Overhead

Steve is a bit of an airline freak, so he loves looking up at the contrails of jets flying overhead and wondering where a plane might be going. He recently found out that Wolfram Alpha can tell you what airplanes are cruising around above you based on your position and its knowledge of where various airline and charter flights are located at any point in time. Because Siri has the built-in capability to work with Wolfram Alpha, he thought he'd see whether he could just ask Siri to tell him about those flights overhead.

It took a few tries and some thought about what to ask Siri, but he finally got it to work. Telling Siri to "Ask Wolfram what flights are overhead" produces the correct results. That query displays a Wolfram Alpha output showing the flight or aircraft registration number of flights that are currently visible from where you're standing, their altitude, and the angle above the horizon. You see this in the Figure 2-9 screenshots. You also get information on what type of aircraft each is, how far away it is, and what direction to look, as well as a sky map showing where the planes are.

Steve then made an attempt to coax details out of Siri about individual flights. He thought he would need to use the brains of Wolfram Alpha again, but found that by simply saying "Tell me about [name of airline] flight [flight number]" prompted Siri to display a web page showing the departure airport and time of the flight along with the expected arrival airport, time, and gate.

The search isn't perfect, with flights between the West Coast and Asia showing up on the search despite the fact that there was no way that the flights were going to be flying over Colorado. But as with many of the tricks Siri can do, this feature shows the surprising depth of knowledge that you have access to by asking Siri.

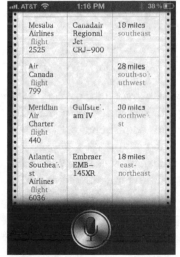

Figure 2-9
Use Siri and Wolfram Alpha to determine which planes are flying above you.

Other Cool Stuff You Can Do with Wolfram Alpha

Here are several ways you can use Siri and Wolfram Alpha to do things that you might not have thought of:

- **Generate a random number:** Tell Siri, "Tell me a random number" or "What is a random number." Wolfram Alpha returns a value between 0 and 1,000.

- **Generate a random password:** Tell Siri, "What is the password." This generates a secure password for you.

- **Check earthquakes:** Tell Siri, "Wolfram, earthquakes," and let Siri find the most recent recorded earthquakes around the world.

- **Graphing equations:** Wolfram Alpha does great graphs and is ready to replace your graphing calculator. Say "Graph Y equals 4x plus 15," for example, or you can also try "What is c over lambda?" This latter is a cool graph, although we were hoping for "Nothing's nu with me. What's nu with you?"

Summary

Siri's powerful capabilities help you search for information through a quick, spoken conversation. In this chapter, you learned about the vast range of topics that Siri can respond to, by working with the built-in iPhone apps, searching the Web, or passing information along to an established search service like Wikipedia or Wolfram Alpha. The points you want to remember from this chapter include the following:

- Siri offers a personal weather assistant, providing information on local conditions or on the other side of the world.

- Siri isn't limited to Google searches. Set your preferences to Google, Yahoo!, or Bing—or choose the search engine you prefer to use by saying its name during your request. It may feel odd to say "Google this," "Bing that," or "Yahoo whatever," but it helps Siri direct your request to the proper engine.

- Don't overlook Wikipedia. It provides another fabulous resource accessible from Siri.

- Siri is your personal stock market reporter. It gives you up-to-date information on individual stocks, markets, and indices, as well as ratios and statistics.

- Wolfram Alpha's integration with Siri offers the most powerful information-gathering combinations on the iPhone 4S. From solving differential equations to telling you what planes are flying overhead, Siri and Wolfram Alpha transform incredible standalone tools into an unbeatable combo together.

Using Siri to Stay in Touch

Siri is the star of the show when it comes to iPhone 4S contacts, helping you to get in touch with others. Siri supercharges the communication capabilities of your iPhone 4S. In this chapter, you learn how to search for contacts, place phone calls, send text messages, and even compose email.

Communication is all about relationships between people, and Siri can learn those relationships for you. You can establish connections between you, your friends and co-workers, and your family. This simplifies contacting others. Just tell Siri who you want to contact, by name or by relationship, and what communication method—phone, text, or email—you want to use.

Pick up your iPhone 4S and prepare to have some fun as you find out how Siri can act as your personal assistant for communicating with the world.

Contacts

When it comes to knowing who your contacts are, Siri provides a direct line into your iPhone address book. For example, it's possible to look up phone numbers, email addresses, birthdays, and other data that you would normally find in the device's Contacts list. You might ask

- What's Victor's address?
- What is Dave Caolo's phone number?
- When is my wife's birthday?
- Show Megan's home email address.

Each query looks up a specific detail for a given contact. Figure 3-1 shows a typical request, asking for the phone number for John Appleseed. After Siri finds that contact for you, tap it to jump into the Address Book application to further view or edit that entry.

Figure 3-1
Siri simplifies looking up specific contact information.

At times, Siri might have trouble distinguishing between contacts with similar names. If you ask, "What is John's phone number?" Siri asks you which John you mean. It does this by presenting a list of possible matches (Figure 3-2). These matches ask the user to specify the intended contact.

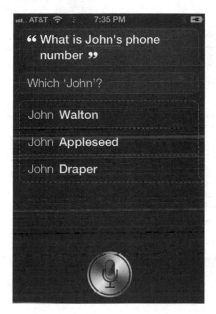

Figure 3-2
Siri might ask you to specify which contact you meant when multiple entries match your request.

To respond to this, tap a name or say the surname out loud—Siri automatically listens whenever it asks you a clarification question. After you've established the contact you meant, Siri enables you to keep referring to John. You won't have to answer any further questions. "Send a text to John" uses the currently selected person's contact information.

If you need to change the context from the current person to another person of the same name, specify the full name (including last name) in your request (for example "Siri, what is John Walton's phone number?"). Siri always tries to remember context, to make each session as seamless as possible. In the case of the address book, that context is the most recently chosen contact.

 NOTE

Nicknames are a great way to differentiate contacts, especially those with common names.

Searching for Contacts

Sometimes you want to view an entire contact entry. Siri helps you to find contacts from your address book. For example, you might ask Siri to "Show Jason Russell" or "Who is Michael Manning?" Each of these queries locates a single person and displays that full contact information (see Figure 3-3).

Once you see what contact information is available, it's easy to use this data to send email, to place phone calls, to write texts, and more.

Figure 3-3
You can view contacts by asking Siri to show them or by asking "Who is."

Relationships

Relationships form an important part of the Siri/address book
story. Although these elements have been part of the address
book programming interface for many years, it hasn't been until
Siri that adding relationships really made important sense on
iOS. That's because Siri enables you to personalize your relationships with others and use those relationships as shortcuts when
making requests.

You can say "Mary Smith is my mother" or "John Appleseed is my friend" (see Figure 3-4) to establish those connections between your contact information and other entries in your address book.

Figure 3-4
Siri creates relationships to connect your contact information to others. You can edit those connections in the Contacts app.

Default relationships include mother, father, parent, sister, brother, child, friend, spouse, partner, manager, and assistant. It's also possible to specify daughter and son, but those are translated automatically to child. Be aware that Exchange in general and

Gmail's version of Exchange do not support all iOS relationships. If you use these, you might not be able to declare those relationships and have them properly update in your Address Book.

Here are some relationship examples you could use with Siri:

- My mom is Susan Islington.
- Michael Fredericks is my brother.
- Call my sister at work.
- Text my assistant.
- Billy Appleseed is my spouse.
- Steve Sande is my friend.
- When is my wife's birthday?
- Emma Sadun is my child.

Each relationship is stored in the standard Contacts application, where you can edit away any inadvertent relationships you might have added by mistake (for example, "Justin Bieber is my husband"—yeah right, smart-aleck daughter who got access to your iPhone).

Creating an Alternative Identity for Yourself

Perhaps you've heard the joke. You tell Siri, "Call me an ambulance," and Siri responds, "From now on, I'll call you, 'An Ambulance,' Okay?" Leanna Lofte pointed out in a great write-up over at iMore (http://imore.com) that this joke is actually of practical use.

It's possible to create a more friendly identity for yourself by telling Siri to call you by your nickname or simply indulge your monomaniacal streak by instructing it to call you "master" or "emperor" or similar (see Figure 3-5).

Figure 3-5
Siri can assign your nickname on demand.

Siri does this by checking out two fields in your primary Contacts entry. The Nickname field takes priority. When you say, "Call me [followed by some name]," Siri updates your Nickname field. Another way to achieve the same result, without adding a nickname to your entry, is to use the phonetic guides.

The Phonetic First Name and Phonetic Last Name fields have been around for quite a while in the Address Book application on both iOS and OS X. They help you pronounce people's names while calling them. For example, you might enter "Ser Hee Yo" for a contact named Sergio, referring to that pronunciation as you're placing your call. (You can also add free-form notes in each contact for other cultural hints.) Siri now uses those fields to override the default pronunciation of your name, as well.

To add these fields in iOS, tap Edit, scroll down to Add Field, and then choose one of the phonetic options.

Pronouncing Your Name

If Siri doesn't seem to pronounce your name the way it should, use these same phonetic fields to give it speaking hints. Enter your name the way it should sound ("Sandy" instead of "Sande," for example); this gives Siri the information it needs to address you correctly.

Save some time by speaking the proper pronunciation into the field. That works great if your name is Sande. It works less great if your name is Sadun (proper pronunciation in America is suh'Doon, or in Italy it is SAAAH-doon).

If your name does not break down into common English words, you're going to end up with nonsense in that field or nothing at all. Just type it in, and help Siri know exactly to say your name.

Placing Phone Calls with Siri

Siri uses your address book contact information to simplify the way you place phone calls. For example, you might say one of the following phrases to initiate calls with one of your personal contacts. If a person is not listed in your address book, just explicitly speak out the number.

- Call Jason.
- Call Biffster. (Yes, Siri works with nicknames, too.)
- Call Jennifer Wright mobile.
- Call Susan on her work phone.
- Call 408-555-1212.
- Call home.
- FaceTime Lisa.

Be aware that Siri does not confirm phone calls before placing them (see Figure 3-6, left). It initiates the call directly and immediately switches to the phone (or FaceTime) application. You can cancel the call in that application as needed but can use an airtime minute in the process. Alternatively, press the Home button before control passes to the Phone application.

Figure 3-6
Siri places calls directly without requiring confirmation (left). If Siri cannot match the destination phone to a contact number (for example you asked to call home but there's no home number), it tries to use another number instead (right).

When contacts offer several phone numbers, you can help Siri by specifying which number to use. For example, you might say, "Call John Appleseed at work" or "Call John Appleseed at home." If Siri cannot exactly match your request to a given number, it tries to offer you an alternative.

In Figure 3-6 (right), John Appleseed's contact entry contains just one phone number, one that's labeled as Mobile. If you ask to call him at home, Siri suggests the mobile number as an alternative. You can confirm using the mobile number or cancel by pressing the Home button.

NOTE

At the time of this writing, you cannot use Siri to dial 911.

Text Messages

The Siri voice assistant on your iPhone 4S helps you use your voice to check your messages, reply to them, and start new conversations. With Siri, you can perform many of your iMessage tasks from anywhere on your iPhone.

Siri supports sending or receiving three different types of messages—standard SMS text messages, MMS multimedia (pictures and video) messages, and Apple's new iMessage format. iMessage bypasses the traditional phone-based messaging system and instead transfers text and multimedia messages over the Internet.

Siri, like the proverbial honey badger, really doesn't care how the messages are sent. It chooses the correct transport method, and ensures that your message is properly dictated and sent to the recipient. One nice feature of iMessage is that it lets you know when the message has been delivered, and it also shows you if someone is in the process of typing a reply.

Reading Texts

Siri loves to read your new text messages to you. This is very useful if you're walking or running somewhere and receive a message that you want to hear. How do you do it? Just ask!

When new messages arrive, tell Siri, "Read my new messages." If you want to hear it another time, tell Siri, "Read it again." Siri fills you in on all the new messages while keeping your hands free for other tasks.

You can reply to your messages in a variety of ways. When you listen to a message, Siri knows what conversation you're in the middle of. This context allows you to say, "Reply, that's great news" or "Tell him I'll be there in a few minutes." If the matter is urgent, just say, "Call her," and Siri uses the contact information associated with the message you just received to look up the user's phone number.

Replying to Texts

After Siri reads you the message, you can use it to reply to the messages hands free. That's perfect for those situations where you might need to respond to an urgent message while driving. Here's what you need to say to Siri:

- Reply that's great news.
- Tell him I'll be there in 10 minutes.
- Call her.

Sending Messages

Siri listens for some key words before sending a text message—*tell*, *send a message*, or *text*—although there may be other terms that it understands. Figure 3-7 shows an example of a message going to Erica.

To create a message, instruct Siri to tell someone something. "Tell Steve, I'll be right there." You can also "text" or "send a message." For example, you could "Send a message to Mike saying 'How about tomorrow?'" or "Text Anthony where are you I have been waiting for 20 minutes." Here are some common phrases to use when telling Siri to dictate and send a message to someone:

- Tell Megan I'll be right there.
- Send a message to Dave Caolo.
- Text Steve and Megs that I'll be a little late.

- Send a message to Paige saying "How about tomorrow?"
- Tell Cathy the birthday present was great.
- Send a message to Susan on her mobile saying I'll feed the dog.
- Send a message to 408-555-1212.
- Text Mike and Victor "Where are you?"

Notice that if you don't have a contact for a person you want to send a message to, but do have his mobile number, you can just tell Siri to send a message to that number. For example, say, "Send a message to 408-555-1212." Siri prompts you for the text contents. Speak your message.

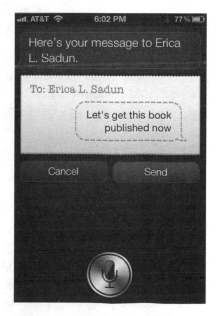

Figure 3-7
When you have an urgent message you need to send to someone, Siri writes it for you, and then asks if you want to send it.

Confirming Messages

Siri asks you to confirm what you said. You reply by asking it to read the message back to you. (Say, "Read it to me" or "Read it back to me.") You can also speak to correct text or mail messages that you have composed. The following examples let Siri know that you're not satisfied with what you've said. Notice that it is possible to change the contents completely, add new material, and so forth:

- Change it to "Let's meet at 3:00 p.m."
- Add, "Can't wait, exclamation point." (You can do this, by the way, even if Siri doesn't mention it explicitly as an option.)
- No, send it to Megs.
- No. (This keeps the message without sending it.)
- Cancel.

When you are satisfied with your text or email message, say something like "Yes, send it" to start the delivery of the message.

Mail

Siri offers a totally new way of sending and reading email and text messages that have been sent to you. No longer do you need to hunt and peck on the iPhone keyboard to assemble an email.

Creating Mail

The proper way to ask Siri to create a blank mail message that is addressed to someone in your Contacts list and add a subject to that message is to say "Email [name or nickname] about [subject]." Telling Siri to "Email Erica about book cover" produces the following conversation (see Figure 3-8).

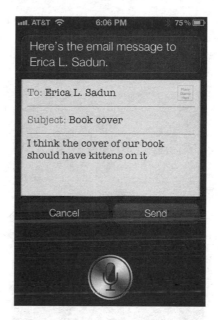

Figure 3-8
Part of a conversation with Siri to write and send an email. The cover of this book may or may not have kittens on it.

At this point, Siri asks what you want the email to say. This enables the dictation function, and Siri listens attentively as you speak your email.

For those people who don't have a nickname, use their first and last names (for example, Erica Sadun) to pull up an email address. Of course, if you have more than one email address for a person, Siri prompts you to select one.

You can shortcut the question and response process in creating an email by telling Siri to "Mail contact about subject and say message." As an example, you could say, "Mail Mom and Dad about

Barb's hospital stay and say thank you for sending the flowers, period, they were lovely, exclamation point." That seeming rambling comment creates a ready-to-send message that looks like the one shown in Figure 3-9.

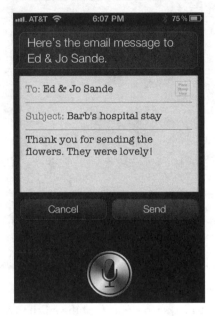

Figure 3-9
This email was addressed, given a subject, and written, all with one long phrase directed at Siri.

Checking Mail

Siri is not a one-trick pony when it comes to working with the Mail app. It can also check your incoming mail and display it on your iPhone screen, although it cannot read it to you aloud. Here are some sample phrases you can try with Siri:

- Check email
- Any new email from Kelly today?
- Show new mail about the wedding.
- Show the email from Nik yesterday.

At this point in time, Siri responds to any request to delete emails with a terse "I'm not allowed to delete emails for you" message.

Responding to Mail

When reading an email message, responding to it with Siri can take several forms. To send a Mail response, say something like "Reply 'Dear Mom, thanks for sending the flowers to the hospital.'" Want to call the person who sent you email? Just say, "Call [him/her/name] at [work/home/iPhone]." Siri dials the phone number of the person, and within seconds you're responding in person to their message.

Sending Mail to a Group

Unfortunately, Mail on the iPhone doesn't have a built-in way to send email to groups. That can be annoying if you need to send messages to a group on a frequent basis, because you have to say something like "Email Tom Shelly and Debby Kinsella and Nancy Brown and Mary Behnke about the bulletin" each and every time you want to send that group a message.

Shortly after the release of the iPhone 4S, we received a message from a company named Soluble Apps (http://solubleapps.com) about a product called MailShot. MailShot provides a way for you to create groups on your iPhone 4S that are accessible from Siri. Figure 3-10 shows this app in action.

Figure 3-10
Using MailShot to create a group mailing list on the iPhone. Speaking the term "Email TUAW Leads about weekend assignments" begins the composition of a message to the group.

In the app, you create MailShot groups that are then added to your Contacts list. Siri understands those group names, so it's possible to send a group email with just a single Siri command. Expect to see even more integration between Siri and other iPhone apps as the intelligent assistant matures.

Friends

Find My Friends is a new iOS 5 utility that you can download from the App Store. This app gives your current location to anyone who you give approval to. Likewise, you can ask your friends with iPhones running iOS 5 to offer you access to their locations. Siri and Find My Friends make it easy to find out where your friends and relatives are at any point and time.

To find those folks, you don't need to launch Find My Friends. Just ask Siri, and it'll tell you the location of a particular person or all of your friends by displaying a map (see Figure 3-11).

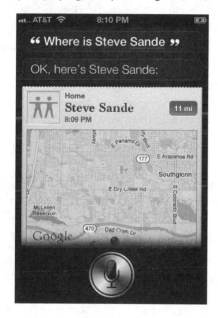

Figure 3-11
Friends who have given you permission to know their location and who have their iPhones turned on can be located with a single Siri command.

You can use quite a few Siri phrases to check the whereabouts of your buddies. Here are some examples that demonstrate friend-finding capabilities:

- Where's Jason? (Useful to know, especially if Jason wears a hockey mask or if you're supposed to meet him for lunch and he's running 15 minutes late. Seeing Jason still driving down the interstate is a major clue that he might have hit some traffic.)

- Where is my sister? (You can use relationship names with Find My Friends, just as you do for making phone calls or texting.)

- Is my wife at home? (If so, don't bring your girlfriend home with you!)

- Where are all my friends? (If they're running away from you, you might want to cut down on all that garlic.)

- Who is here? (We can't wait to use that when we're at Macworld/iWorld, or anywhere else where we can catch up with Internet buddies whom we might not have met in person.)

- Who is near me?

Just remember, Siri won't know where your friends are if you haven't set them up with Find My Friends first. Use the app to send invitations to your closest friends and relatives who all have iOS 5 on their iPhone, iPod touch, or iPad.

Also be aware that you need to log in to Find My Friends to use the service with Siri. Once you do, you'll be authorized for a good long period. If you pull out your iPhone while driving and immediately expect to find people, you might be disappointed. Always try to log in before heading to the car if you expect to use this feature.

Summary

Your iPhone 4s and Siri are better communicators than those devices you remember from *Star Trek*. Sure, the iPhone 4S isn't as small as those cool badge communicators on the later

generations of *Star Trek*, but your device can not only call someone at your voice command, but also send text messages and
emails. Plus you won't get bruises from hitting your chest all the
time. Throw in some of the non-Siri communication capabilities,
such as FaceTime or Twitter, and you have an extremely powerful
communication tool.

Several things you should take away from this chapter include the
following points:

- Relationships, especially unique ones, simplify your life when
  using Siri. If your spouse has a common name like John or
  Barbara or Steve, referring to him or her as my wife or my husband helps jump you past the hurdles of figuring out which
  John, Barbara, or Steve you are referring to. Take advantage
  of the spouse/assistant/child/parent relationships to speed up
  texts, emails, and calls to important persons in your life.

- The Contacts app on the iPhone 4S provides tight Siri integration. Information about a contact's phone numbers, addresses,
  email addresses and more is just a question away.

- Use Siri voice commands for calling, emailing, and texting
  people in your contacts. For email and text, use the dictation
  commands from Chapter 7, "Dictation," to create complete
  messages with proper punctuation. You can dictate and send
  text and email messages with just your voice.

- Siri reads your incoming text messages to you, but cannot
  yet read full email messages. This is a feature we're looking
  forward to in future Siri updates. To reply to messages, just tell
  Siri to answer it, and then dictate your reply.

- You cannot yet send emails to a Contact list group without
  third-party software. Groups created using MailShot are currently addressable via Siri, letting you contact work or family
  groups through a single message.

Talking to Your Day-Timer

For many people, an iPhone or other smartphone provides a replacement for a handwritten organizer like the classic Day-Timer. If you're too young to be familiar with Day-Timers, they have printed pages with spaces for reminders, notes, and calendar appointments, as well as lists of contacts.

Rather than scrawling handwritten notes onto a printed calendar page, the iPhone 4S and Siri set up appointments, take notes, and set reminders with a conversation. It's more like having your own personal assistant taking care of business for you than using an electronic device.

This chapter introduces you to the ways you can use Siri to help schedule and organize your life. It's time to throw away that handwritten organizer.

Calendars

If you've owned an iPhone before, you might already be a fan of the Calendar app for keeping track of your appointments and meetings. With Siri, you'll feel like you have your own concierge at your beck and call, handling all of your calendar events. Through the magic of iCloud, any calendar events you make with Siri are immediately synchronized to any other devices you might have connected to the service.

Adding Events

Adding an event using Siri follows a standard conversational pattern. You tell it to "Set up a meeting," "Meet with someone," "Schedule a meeting," or "Make an appointment" with one or more people at a certain date or time. Figure 4-1 shows this approach in action.

Many times when setting up a meeting, you'll want an alert a few minutes before it starts. This helps you remember to participate. Unfortunately, there doesn't appear to be a way at this time to tell Siri to add an alert to a calendar event. To add an alert and specify the sound to use when the alert is made, you need to use reminders, which we discuss in the next section. Reminders play an alert tone by default.

You might want to create a calendar event for a meeting to block out time on your calendar and send invitations to others, and then make a reminder to alert you before the start of the meeting.

Figure 4-1
Asking Siri to set up a meeting with one person or more at a specific time and location creates a calendar entry with all the pertinent information filled in.

In real life, meetings and appointments have a tendency to change. That's fine; Siri is amenable to making changes. Here are some phrases you might use to change an event on your calendar:

- Move my 10 a.m. meeting to 2:30. (Siri will know the meeting is for 2:30 p.m.)

- Reschedule my appointment with Dr. Hathaway to next Monday at 9 a.m.

- Add Erica to my meeting with Apple.

- Cancel the final book review meeting.

- Change the location of my 3 p.m. meeting tomorrow to Bob's office.

NOTE

Siri uses your contacts information to derive location names. The physical address you entered in Bob's address book entry for work is used here to evaluate "Bob's office." Siri uses location-based services when you enable Settings, Location Services and set the switch for Siri to ON.

Checking Your Calendar

Many times you might just want to find out something about a meeting, like what time and date it is scheduled for, where the meeting is, or what you've got scheduled for a specific day. Never fear, Siri's here! A quick conversation with Siri is like asking a human assistant to look at your calendar for you (see Figure 4-2).

Figure 4-2
Need to know what's coming up on your agenda for tomorrow? Ask Siri and you get an immediate answer.

Calendar Queries

What kind of calendar-related questions can you ask Siri? Here are several examples of statements you might use to ask Siri about upcoming events on your calendar:

- What does the rest of my day look like?
- What's on my calendar for Wednesday?
- When is my next appointment?
- When am I meeting with Erica?
- Where is my next meeting?

When your meeting doesn't have a location, Siri tells you that it doesn't know where the meeting is to be held. Siri's pretty smart, so it also responds with an "I don't think you have any meetings with [whomever]" in those situations where you mistakenly think you've set up a meeting with someone—but really haven't.

Siri can also tell you the date for an upcoming or past day of the week. For example, if you ask, "What date was last Thursday?" Siri responds with an answer like "It was Thursday, October 13, 2011." Even more impressive, you can ask, "What day of the week was December 7, 1941" (or any other date), and you'll get an answer.

Reminders

Reminders are different from calendar events. Think of reminders, which are accessed through the Reminders app on your iPhone 4S, as an intelligent to-do list. Reminders usually have a date and time associated with them (think of this as a deadline for completing a task), or you can use the Geofencing features of your iPhone 4S to remind you of something when you arrive at or leave a location.

Figure 4-3 shows a typical conversation with Siri to set up a rather complex reminder, in this case to help you remember to take your medicine.

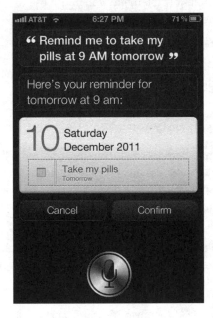

Figure 4-3
This phrase tells Siri to remind you to take needed medicines tomorrow morning. People are notoriously forgetful and Siri isn't.

How Siri Can Remind You

Here are examples of some of the other things you can say to Siri to have it remind you of things:

- Remind me to call Mom.
- Remind me to call Mom when I get home.
- Remember to take an umbrella.

- Remind me to take my medicine at 6 a.m. tomorrow.
- Remind me to find an ATM when I leave here.
- Remind me when I leave to call Jason.
- Remind me to buy milk every 4 days.
- Remind me to finish the report by 6 p.m.
- Remind me to park outside when I arrive at Bob's house.
- Remind me to join the conference call every Wednesday at 3 p.m.

The last conversation here is an example of setting up a recurring reminder. You can ask Siri to remind you every day, every week, every two weeks, once a month, or once a year. Now there's no excuse for forgetting your anniversary, guys!

A Word of Caution

One word of caution when using the geolocation-based reminders: This enables Location Services for the Reminders app. A small white arrow on the iPhone status bar next to the battery indication is your cue that your iPhone 4S is actively finding your current location. Why should you be concerned? Location Services is notorious for causing higher-than-average power use, resulting in shorter battery life. The reminders are great. The shorter-than-expected battery life might not be.

Creating Notes

Siri makes it easy to add quick hands-free notes on your iPhone. You can't beat the convenience of getting tiny tidbits of information recorded with a single tap and chat. Here are some additional ways you can use this handy feature.

Creating Single-Item Notes

It's easy to add single-item notes, like "Note that I spent $5 on parking" (see Figure 4-4) or "Note: Check out that new Parry Grip compilation album." Each of these spoken commands creates a single standalone note item in the Notes application.

Figure 4-4
Siri easily creates single item notes.

Adding Items to the Current Note

Siri retains context, so you can add items to the currently edited note, one at a time. The key word here is *add*. For example, say "Add do laundry" and Siri adds *do laundry* to the current note. Alternatively, say "Add" or "Add to note." Siri responds, "What would you like to add?" and automatically starts listening for a response. Each time, you add one item to the current note, so you expand the note as needed. Figure 4-5 shows how to create and then add to a note.

Figure 4-5
Use "add" commands to add items to the current note.

Starting New Notes

When you want to start a new note rather than add to an existing one, just tell Siri, "Take a note" or "Start a note"—or just use the one-sentence "Note that… something…" structure. If you don't provide contents, Siri responds with "OK, I can take that note for you… just tell me what you want it to say," at which point you use "Add a note" to keep adding to that new note.

Naming Notes

To name notes, refer to the first item added to them. For example, you can "Create a 'do this' note" and then add notes to that by saying "Add buy milk to my 'do this' note." Figure 4-6 shows an example of using a named list to add items.

Figure 4-6
Creating and adding notes. Tap on any note to view it in the Notes application.

Finding Notes

Retrieve the note by asking Siri to find it. Figure 4-7 shows the response of "Find my 'do this' note." Unfortunately, you cannot ask Siri to "Read it to me." Siri only reads incoming text messages at this time. Instead, Siri displays the note it finds on the screen for your reading pleasure.

Figure 4-7
Siri retrieves notes by title, which corresponds to the first line in each note.

Viewing All Notes

Telling Siri "Show me my notes" or "Show me all the notes" displays all your notes as a table of contents.

 NOTE

Unfortunately, Siri does not offer any note editing features other than adding items. You cannot delete notes without going into the Notes application.

Clock Functions

Siri is nicely integrated with the clock functions of the iPhone. The usual clock functions that are built in to the iPhone's firmware include an alarm clock, a countdown timer, a world clock displaying the current time in locations around the globe, and a stopwatch. Siri doesn't want to be a stopwatch when it grows up, but it will happily serve you in the other clock functions.

Alarms

You know how it is when you're trying to set an alarm clock. Usually you press the little button and watch the wake time spin past, and then you have to do it all over again. It's easier on the iPhone; you just spin the hour and minute you want to wake up to set an alarm. As expected, Siri makes setting an alarm a matter of talking to your iPhone and telling it when you want that alarm to go off. Figure 4-8 shows an extreme example of a conversation with Siri asking it to wake you up the next morning.

Other Ways to Set Alarms

You can also to talk Siri into doing your bidding to set up, change, or delete alarms in other ways. Here are some standard conversations:

- Wake me up tomorrow at 7 a.m.
- Set an alarm for 6:30 p.m.
- Wake me up in 8 hours.
- Change my 6:30 alarm to 6:45.
- Turn off my 6:30 alarm.
- Delete my 7:30 alarm.

Figure 4-8
Siri understands the "wake me at 9 a.m. tomorrow" and sets an alarm. The "whoa dude" is totally ignored by the brilliant and friendly Siri.

How do you know what sound your iPhone is going to use to wake you from your sweet dreams? It uses whatever alarm tone you have used previously, or you can tap on the Alarm button of the Clock app, tap the Edit button, and then select a sound. Sadly, Siri doesn't come with a snooze command—it won't listen as you plead for "just 10 more minutes" of sleep. Perhaps the next version of Siri will provide that capability.

World Clock

When it comes to the world clock functions of Siri, you can start with your little part of the world. Siri knows where you are, and responds to a query of "What time is it?" by telling you the local time.

That's the least of its capabilities, however. When you need to know whether it's a good time to call your business partner in Mumbai, all you need to do is ask what time it is there (see Figure 4-9).

Figure 4-9
The world clock capabilities of Siri enable you to determine the time for most major cities around the world.

Using a Timer

Our families love cooking outside on the grill, and one of the key success factors we've discovered in our outdoor cooking is to use a timer to let us know when to flip the food, take meat off the heat, or let it rest. Since Siri has entered our lives, setting a timer can now be done one handed. Press the Home button, bring the iPhone to your ear, and say "Set a timer for 7 minutes," and you get verification from Siri that the timer is counting down.

Timers can also be paused, resumed, or stopped. Here are examples of using Siri to set timers:

- Set the timer for 10 minutes.
- Show the timer.
- Pause the timer.
- Resume.
- Reset the timer.

Siri uses whatever timer alert sound has been set under the Timer tab of the Clock app. You select your favorite ear-shattering noise by tapping the When Timer Ends button. If you'd like to know how much longer the timer has to go, just ask Siri, "What's the timer status?"

Summary

With Siri working overtime on your iPhone 4S, it's like having a personal assistant who works for you wherever and whenever you want. Through easy, natural-language statements, Siri sets appointments, checks your calendar, and sets and announces reminders.

Siri is also an incredible help with time functions. Whether you need to set an alarm to wake yourself up, set a duration timer for cooking, or find the correct time anywhere in the world, a quick conversation gets the job done. Here are some things to take away from this chapter:

- Adding an appointment to your calendar represents just one task Siri performs. Remember that you can work with Siri to find out your next appointment, determine what your calendar looks like for a certain day, and change meeting attendees, times, and locations through verbal commands.

- Reminders are different from appointments in that they are more like a to-do list that can have a deadline. You can also set Siri to remind you of something when you arrive at or leave somewhere using geofencing features. Your iPhone then monitors your location and triggers those reminders when you approach or leave a tagged destination.

- People who like to annotate their lives with handwritten Post-it Notes will love Siri's ability to create and add to lists through speech. Imagine dictating a shopping list to your iPhone 4S as you drive to a store, and you have a good idea of the power of Siri's interactions with notes.

- Interacting with the iPhone 4S clock no longer requires hands-on action. Instead, ask Siri to set, change, or delete an alarm; start or stop a timer; or tell you what time it is in any major city of the world.

Going Shopping with Siri

In our busy twenty-first-century lives, time is a precious commodity. Siri helps you make the best of your limited free time by helping you to search for goods and services, find your way to local businesses, and even calculate tips and taxes.

This chapter explores the ways that Siri works at your command to make your shopping journeys as smooth as possible. Siri hunts down the items you crave, and reminds you to buy something when you are near a store that carries an item. Siri in your pocket acts like an invisible assistant whose sole goal in life is to get you out of stores and back to enjoying friends, family, and that ever-shrinking free time.

Products and Services

Siri provides an amazing interface for hunting down products and services. You might say to Siri, "I'm in the mood for Italian food," and Siri will try to find exactly what you're looking for based on your current location (see Figure 5-1). Just tap on any of the offerings to find directions and phone numbers.

Figure 5-1
Siri finds restaurants, stores, services, and more, all with simple queries.

Typical Shopping Requests

Siri loves to track down many types of goods and services for you. Shopping requests you might make include the following:

- Find me a bike shop.
- Where can I go to read a book?

- I'm looking for a health clinic.
- What's a good place for dinner?
- Is there a dentist near me?
- How far is it from here to a library?
- I want to buy clothing.
- Remind me to pick up a 12-pack of soda when I leave work.
- Where can I buy milk?

As Figure 5-2 shows, Siri often sorts items by rating for you, simplifying your search. Other times, Siri's searches will show closer items first. You can't always know when the sorting will happen for each query, but when they do, they're always set up to simplify the task you've asked Siri about.

Figure 5-2
Siri may sort some of its searches by rating, enabling you to scan the best-rated items first.

Checking Prices

Siri can look up prices for you for certain commodities, such as gasoline, bread, potatoes, ground beef, butter, eggs, orange juice, sugar, and milk. You can also look at average prices of toothpaste, facial tissues, shampoo, detergent, dry cleaning, haircuts, movie tickets, newspapers, and bowling, among other standard items. For example, you might ask Siri, "What is the average price of a gallon of gasoline in Denver?" (see Figure 5-3) or "How much does milk cost in Denver?" In addition to pricing in big cities, Siri also provides prices on a state or national level. Siri cannot, however, look up shelf prices at the local grocery, so you can see only averages. What's more, Siri cannot look for vendors based on price ranges, so you cannot ask, "Where is the cheapest gas station near me?" or "Where can I find inexpensive groceries?"

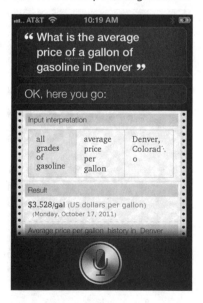

Figure 5-3
Siri enables you to check average prices on certain commodities.

Adding Sales Tax

Siri can help you shop by calculating sales tax. Just ask how much a purchase is with tax added for a given city, as shown in Figure 5-4 (left). This is a great way to calculate your final purchase price.

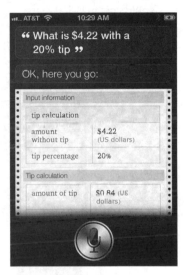

Figure 5-4
Siri calculates sales tax and tip for you.

Want to add a tip? Siri does that, too (see Figure 5-4, right). Siri does calculate the total with tip as well as the amount of tip as separate listings, but the iPhone 4S will not show both the question and the results with that all on one screen. To see the amount with tip, as well as the amount with standard tips like 10%, 15%, 20%, and 25%, just scroll down the results.

Currency Conversion

If you are traveling abroad or purchasing from overseas mer-
chants, Siri can help you convert between currencies. As Figure
5-5 shows, Siri converts currencies to show you what a purchase
would cost in U.S. dollars.

Figure 5-5
Converting between currencies helps you shop abroad or from foreign websites.

Preparing a Shopping List

Cliff Joyce of Pure Blend Software introduced us to our favorite
way of putting together shopping lists in Siri.

Start in the Reminders application and create a new list. To do
this, tap the Lists button at the top-left corner of the application.

It looks like three lines on top of each other. Then tap Edit, Create New List, and enter the name **Groceries**. Click Done. After you have a list named Groceries (see Figure 5-6), you can refer to it in Siri.

Figure 5-6
When you create lists in the Reminders app, you can refer to them by name in Siri.

After you create the list, add items to it with simple requests whenever you think of something new you need to buy. Tell Siri, "Add eggs to my Groceries list." Siri asks you to confirm the new item (see Figure 5-7). Just say "yes," and Siri adds it for you. When you're at the market, just check off the items as you buy them. It couldn't be easier.

Figure 5-7
Siri can add items to your list whenever you run out of them in your pantry. Just tell it to add the new item and confirm.

This add-to-reminders approach is also, by the way, an amazing way for people on diets to keep food logs. Siri's Wolfram Alpha integration makes it possible to look up calorie content for a large variety of foods. Between Wolfram and reminders, Siri is the perfect diet-logging tool.

 NOTE

Mark Johnson, an Australian Siri user, provides this hint: "In Australia, Siri seems to not hear 'Add' very well. Despite lots of attempts to harden the consonant, it keeps thinking I am saying 'and eggs to the shopping list,' and then tries to find a business (which isn't supported here). I have found that 'put eggs on my shopping list' works really well, however."

Sharing Reminders with the Cloud

Lex Friedman of Macworld came up with a remarkably clever way to share reminder lists with others. Log in to iCloud.com and enter the Calendar section. Click the gear icon (top right), New Reminder List. The new list appears in the list on the left side of the screen. Double-click the list and edit its name (for example, Cloud).

To add people to the reminders list, click the small Wi-Fi-esque signal icon to the right of its name. Add each person by email address. Click Share to finish. Each person receives a confirmation email. If you plan to share your reminders only with highly trusted people, such as your spouse, you can share your default reminders list (called Reminders) using these steps, without creating a new one.

By adding people to your shared list, you enable them to see your reminders in their iCloud and iCal lists in the iOS Reminders app. Then, all you have to do is tell Siri, "Add pickup the library books to my cloud list."

Friedman points out this killer use for shared lists. He writes, "Add your local supermarket as a contact in your iPhone address book, and of course add its address. (I called mine 'The Supermarket.') Now, you can say, 'Remind me to buy eggs when I get to the supermarket'; when you—or whomever you've shared your list with—arrives at the supermarket, Reminders will, well, remind you—or whomever—about the item(s) on your list."

Shopping Limitations

Siri doesn't always get your shopping requests right. It has been optimized for a general urban lifestyle and may miss the subtleties localized to, for example, living in Denver, home to the National

Western Stock Show, where you can, in fact, easily buy a cow, a pig, a sheep, and so forth (see Figure 5-8).

Figure 5-8
Siri, clearly, does not live in Colorado. Yee-haw.

Maps

Siri offers amazing integration with the Maps app on your iPhone 4S. Just this morning, we asked Siri to find an ATM near us, and within seconds we had a map in front of us with a sprinkling of red pins designating all money machines within a few mile radius of our location.

Of course, you have to look at the iPhone screen to see where everything is, so the combination of Siri and Maps is not a very good replacement for a turn-by-turn navigation app—yet. We can't wait until that functionality ships in a future version of Siri itself or via application integration with TomTom, Navigon, or some other turn-by-turn app.

One common use case for Siri and Maps is finding out where certain businesses are near your present location or an area where you might be traveling. Here are some examples of how you might use Siri to locate vendors (see Figure 5-9).

Figure 5-9
Hungry for a good burger? Siri gives you a list of the best restaurants of a specific type, listed by Yelp review ranking.

- Find coffee near me.
- Where is the nearest McDonalds?
- Find some pizza restaurants in Taos, New Mexico.
- Where's a gas station within walking distance?
- Where's an ATM around here?

When Siri finds a business or list of businesses, just tap on one of them to see a map showing the surroundings. A tap on the red

pin that pinpoints the business displays an information page with
information like the address and phone number, as well as but-
tons to get directions to or from the place.

It's also possible to ask Siri for directions directly. This is helpful if
you're in an unfamiliar neighborhood and want to get home—just
ask Siri "How do I get home?" and a Google map showing up to
three alternative routes appears on the screen (see Figure 5-10).

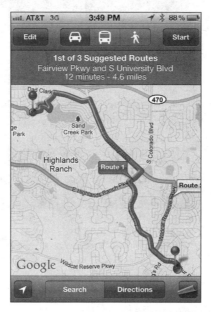

Figure 5-10
While trying to get home, Siri displays three different routes, along with estimated trip durations,
distances, and the major thoroughfares traveled. Tap the Start button to begin seeing turn-by-turn
directions. You can tap on each route to highlight it.

As Figure 5-10 shows, just tap the Start button to view the turn-
by-turn directions. At this early stage of the life of Siri, it doesn't

read the directions to you. Other direction-related commands that Siri understands are as follows:

- Show 1 Infinite Loop, Cupertino, California.
- Directions to Barb's office.
- How do I get to Taco Bell?

Siri is quite useful in terms of finding businesses and directions. Just remember not to use the maps functionality while you're driving, because you will need to interact with your iPhone screen. Let your passenger help out, or pull over to get those directions from Siri.

 NOTE

We can't wait until Apple offers developers Siri API integration. This will allow third-party developers to integrate Siri requests into their apps. Some day, telling Siri "Take me home" will allow your favorite navigation app to provide the same turn-by-turn vocal directions they do now, but do so via a Siri request.

Summary

As you've seen in this chapter, Siri can help you shop for goods and services with a few well-chosen words. Whether you're looking for a specific type of restaurant or store, checking average prices for commodities, preparing a shopping list, or just trying to get directions to or from a store, Siri has the answer.

When using Siri to simplify your shopping trips, here are some things to keep in mind:

- Siri's search results are often sorted by distance from your current location for stores, and restaurants are sorted by the rating they've achieved on Yelp.

- Siri can look up average prices for certain commodities in your area like milk and gasoline, but it can't tell you the prices of specific items at a particular store.

- Purchasing something in another currency? Ask Siri to calculate how much the item costs in your local currency—but watch out for those expensive data roaming charges if you're off your usual mobile carrier's network.

- Need to write a shopping list? You don't have to drag out a piece of paper and a pencil. Create a special list in Reminders, and then tell Siri what to add to the list. You can share your shopping list with others through iCloud, and set it up to remind you to pick up items when you're near a store.

- Let Siri do the math. Why drag out the Calculator app when Siri splits tabs, calculates tips, and figures out how much everything costs with tax added?

- Although Siri excels at finding directions to and from locations, at this early date it won't yet give you turn-by-turn verbal instructions. This is another feature we're hoping to see in future updates.

Pushing Limits with Siri

Like the universe in which we live, the Siri universe continues to expand over time. Although Apple has not yet given developers a way to tap the power of Siri in third-party apps, the millions of early adopters have been able to come up with some very clever uses for the intelligent assistant.

Bloggers and fans of Twitter are finding that they can use Siri's text messaging capabilities with SMS-enabled services to post new content to their blogs or tweet about what's happening. Music aficionados have found that Siri works with the iPhone Music app to select and play songs, or even find out the name and artist of a song that is playing.

In this chapter, you also find information about how to keep your iPhone secure when using Siri. After that rather dark subject, we lighten up your day with a list of all the things you can ask Siri to evoke a clever and sometimes hysterically funny response. It turns out that your personal assistant has quite an intentional (and sometimes unintentional) sense of humor.

Connecting Siri with Services: Tweeting and Blogging

At this time, although we're pretty sure this will change in the near future, Siri cannot tweet directly (see Figure 6-1), or connect with Google+, or interface with many other similar services. That functionality just isn't built in yet.

Figure 6-1
Siri does not yet support tweeting (at least through official channels). You can use Siri's SMS messaging support to make an end run to Tweeting support.

Tweeting

This doesn't mean you can't work around this limitation. Twitter has built-in support (see https://support.twitter.com/articles/14226-how-to-find-your-twitter-short-code-or-long-code) for sending updates by SMS.

Create a Twitter contact in your address book and add its SMS code (40404 in the United States). Send a text (using Siri or otherwise) with the word *start*. This allows you to begin the process of associating your username and credentials with your phone number. Once established, you can use Siri to tweet via SMS.

Note that SMS text messaging rates apply, which means that you might spend anywhere from 10 cents to 25 cents per tweet. If you just want to tweet directly, consider launching your favorite Twitter app, create a blank tweet, and then tap the microphone icon on the virtual keyboard to dictate your tweet.

Blogging

Did you know that you could create blog posts entirely by voice? We're not talking about basic dictation either. That's because Siri supports SMS messaging, and a little-known feature of Google Blogger enables you to create blog posts entirely by text.

Interested in giving it a spin? Send *register* to 256447. Blogger replies to your registration text by texting you a URL for your new blog and an optional claim code. This code is used to associate your new access with an existing blog. It just as easy, however, to work with the automatically generated blog address that is sent to you.

To create a new post, just reply to the 256447 conversation. Dictate your new blog post to Siri and send it. When you do, the text contents are instantly posted to the blog. Figure 6-2 shows a post created using Siri.

Figure 6-2
Use Siri and Google's blogging-by-SMS service to dictate your blog posts.

If you're on a limited SMS diet, posting by text message may prove too rich for your blood. There's still a Siri-capable workaround for that, but you must use an existing Blogger account to create a Mail-to-Blogger address.

You'll find a complete set of instructions at the Blogger help article on this subject (www.google.com/support/blogger/bin/answer.py?answer=41452). That write-up shows you how to use your account settings to establish your blogging email address, which consists of your username and a secret word.

Other Services

Both Tumblr and Posterous offer SMS access, although they tend to be a bit finicky. You might consider using ping.fm (http://ping.fm) or HelloTXT (http://hellotxt.com) as workarounds for sending updates to these services.

If you prefer not to use Blogger, plenty of other services support blog posting via email. Tumblr, Posterous, WordPress.com, and self-hosted WordPress blogs all support creating a custom address that you use to post directly. You can find signup instructions for these services here:

- www.tumblr.com/docs/en/email_publishing
- http://help.posterous.com/how-to-post-by-email-video
- codex.wordpress.org/Post_to_your_blog_using_email

Just add the email to your address book with a distinctive-yet-pronounceable contact name, and then tell Siri "Send an email to [the service name]" to dictate your post and share it with the world.

Search around for other email and SMS-based services that are usable with Siri and social networks. There are more out there than the few mentioned here.

Music

Although a lot of the built-in Siri support centers on controlling your schedule and finding information, Siri also acts as your personal media DJ. With Siri, you can select music, play it, and control the playback. For example, you might say some of these phrases to choose a music selection.

- Play "The Light of the Sun."
- Play "Trouble."

- Play *Taking Back Sunday* shuffled.
- Play Alicia Keys.
- Play some blues/some country/some rock and roll.
- Play my party mix.
- Shuffle my road-trip playlist.
- Play my Dixie Chicks playlist.
- Shuffle this playlist.
- Play/pause/resume/skip/next song/previous song.
- What is this song?/Who is this song by?

Be aware that Siri fades out any currently playing audio when the assistant interface appears. So when you ask "What is this song?" you won't actually be hearing the song you're asking about.

Siri Security

Almost immediately after the release of the iPhone 4S, we started receiving emails from users who noticed that even when they had a passcode set on the lock screen someone could pick up their device and issue commands to Siri. This means that unauthorized persons could pick up the iPhone 4S, press and hold the Home button, and converse with Siri. Fortunately, you can disable Siri while using a lock screen passcode.

The Sophos Naked Security blog (http://nakedsecurity.sophos.com) notes that unauthorized users can do everything from writing an email or sending a text message to maliciously changing calendar appointments. Blogger Graham Cluely pointed out that it's easy to disable Siri while a passcode is in effect, and wonders why Apple didn't set the iPhone 4S up that way by default.

To make sure Siri is deaf to commands when there's a passcode on the iPhone 4S, enter Settings, General, Passcode Lock, and slide the Siri option to OFF (see Figure 6-3). Now, when your friends try to make a prank call to your girlfriend using your iPhone 4S, they'll find that Siri is unwilling to participate in the prank.

Figure 6-3
Increase your Siri security by disabling the access override.

One further note about security: When you allow Siri access from the lock screen, you also override any Find My Friends privacy. Siri does not prompt you to log in at the lock screen the way it does when using the service normally. This is either a big security hole or a great convenience when you're trying to get together with a friend for lunch. Adjust your usage accordingly.

Having Fun with Siri

You have now read deeply into the practical day-to-day topics of Siri use. You've seen how to check the weather, send text messages, control your playlist, calculate tips, and more. Those things are all well and good, but they fail to showcase Siri's sparkle.

After all, Siri is fun as well as practical. You can use Siri in a, forgive the pun, serious manner and totally miss the point of how delightful a tool it is to use. With that in mind, the following sections introduce the lighter side of Siri.

Siri offers many delightful diversions when you have a few minutes to play around with its features. As Figure 6-4 shows, Siri is quite whimsical if you know how to ask the right questions or feed it the right statement.

Figure 6-4
Siri can do a lot more than you might expect.

You can engage Siri in many ways. Consider the lists of statements that follow. Siri can respond to all of these, often with a silly reply. What's more, Siri can often supply more than one answer for certain statements. Figure 6-5 demonstrates this multiplicity. It's often worth trying again if Siri offers a reply that particularly tickles your funny bone.

Figure 6-5
Siri often has multiple answers ready for fun statements.

The Lighter Side of Siri

Here are some suggestions that help showcase Siri's lighter side. To test them, just engage Siri and speak. You can hold the iPhone to your ear and wait for the beep, or you can press and hold the Home button until Siri activates. Without further ado, and in no particular order, here you go.

Asking About Siri

Your virtual assistant has a lot going on behind the scenes, which you might have to entice out due to Siri's natural reticence and modesty. Here are ways to start getting to know Siri better:

- Who are you?
- What is your name?
- What does *Siri* mean?
- How are you, Siri?
- Why are you so awesome?
- Who is your husband/your wife?
- What are you wearing?
- What is your name?
- How old are you?
- When is your birthday?
- Who is your family? (Who is your mother? Who is your father? Who is your friend?)
- What is your favorite color?
- What do you like?
- What are you doing?
- Who is Eliza?

Siri Chitchat

Siri can provide some chuckles when it responds with pre-canned responses to otherwise basic statements:

- Thank you.
- Have a nice day.
- I love you.

- Why don't you love me?
- You're silly.
- What is the best computer in the world?/What is the best phone in the world?/What is the best tablet?
- What do you think about Android? (Be sure to ask a few times.)
- What's new?
- Testing/Testing 1 2 3.
- Tell me a joke/a story.
- Can you sing?
- Knock knock?
- What is the meaning of life?
- Howdy.
- Hah!/Ye hah!/Ye haha!/ha ha/LOL/ROFL.
- I'm bored.
- Why does my wife/husband hate me?
- Do you want to know a secret?

Pop-Culture Fun

Siri is well versed in some pop-culture references. Here are some that it can respond to directly:

- Open the pod bay doors.
- Do you know HAL 9000?
- I can't let you do that, Dave.
- Klaatu barada nikto.
- Beam me up, Scotty. (Also: Siri, beam me up.)
- Tea. Earl Grey. Hot. (This one isn't super funny, but boy it's fun to be able to say it!)

- Take me to your leader.
- Who is your leader?
- Who's on first?/on second?/on third?

Siri Miscellany

Here are more fun items you can say to Siri, without any specific categories assigned to them:

- Can you murder someone for me? (No really, it's funny. Try it.)
- Where can I hide a body?
- When is Santa Claus coming to town?
- Do you believe in Santa Claus?
- Merry Christmas/Happy New Year/Happy Halloween/Happy Columbus Day (and so on).
- When is Thanksgiving? (Sometimes Siri gives a little extra snark, so be patient.)
- Are you self-aware? (Also: Are you a god?)
- Will you marry me? (Really, keep asking this one. Some of them are hilarious.)
- Siri! Siri! Siri!
- I'm drunk.
- Call me an ambulance.
- I don't like your tone.
- Blah blah blah.
- I have to urinate/poop.
- I am cold.
- I am sleepy.
- What do you think of peace? (Siri used to respond to "What do you think of war?" but It got censored.)

- Siri, can you find email I sent tomorrow?
- (Say the following with nothing playing.) Please don't stop the music.
- Try saying "Good morning" at night or "Good evening" in the morning.
- (This is clean/family safe. Promise!) Talk dirty to me.
- What's the best cell phone network?
- Quit all open applications.

Mining the Fun in Wolfram Alpha

Wolfram Alpha includes a lot of built-in humor. Here are some of the statements that Siri can interpret without having to use the "Ask Wolfram" prefix on your requests:

- How many licks does it take to get to the center of a tootsie pop?
- Does this dress make me look fat?
- How much do you cost?
- How many roads must a man walk down before you can call him a man?
- Why did the chicken cross the road?
- How many angels can dance on the head of a pin?
- Where did I put my keys?
- Who let the dogs out?
- Who shot JFK?
- Who shot JR?
- What is the difference between a duck?
- How long is a piece of string?
- How do I shot web?

- What's the frequency, Kenneth? (Okay, it's not nearly as cool as you might want, but at least Siri properly accepts that as an input.)
- What's the winning Lotto numbers?
- What is a computational knowledge engine?
- Who watches the watchmen?
- Does God exist?
- Who lives in a pineapple under the sea?
- Who's the boss?
- What is the number of the beast?
- Mirror, mirror on the wall, who's the fairest of them all? (Make sure you pause slightly after the word *wall*.)

Queries That Require Wolfram Prefixes

Each of the following items needs a little query love to ensure that Siri directs them properly to Wolfram Alpha. You can use "Wolfram," "Ask Wolfram," or "What is" to ensure they are sent to Wolfram:

- What is "a flux capacitor?"
- What is "88 miles per hour?"
- What is "How is babby formed?"
- What is "Where's Waldo?"
- What is "To be or not to be?"
- What is "Are you self-aware?"
- Wolfram, "Shall we play a game?"
- Wolfram, "Am I pretty?"
- Wolfram, "Are we there yet?"
- Wolfram, "Who ya gonna call?"

- Wolfram, "Are you going to kill all humans?"
- Wolfram, "Hit me!"
- Wolfram, "I know Kung Fu."
- Wolfram, "What do the knights say?"
- Wolfram, "What is your favorite color?"
- Wolfram, "Could a swallow carry a coconut?"
- What is the airspeed velocity of an unladen swallow?
- Wolfram, "Where is Carmen Sandiego?"
- Wolfram, "Why so serious?"
- Wolfram, "Rick roll."
- Wolfram, "Why is the sky blue?"
- Wolfram, "Number of horns on a unicorn?"
- Wolfram, "Can you eat?"
- Wolfram, "Who's afraid of the big bad wolf?"
- Wolfram, "Who framed Roger Rabbit?"
- Wolfram, "What is dilithium?"
- Wolfram, "Who is Luke's father?"
- Wolfram, "Who shot the sheriff?"
- Wolfram, "Were the moon landings faked?"
- Wolfram, "If a tree falls in the forest, does it make a sound?"
- Wolfram, "What is in the box?"
- Wolfram, "What are midi chlorians?"

Summary

Siri's creators knew that people would try to ask the intelligent assistant a lot of silly questions to see if they could stump it. Rather than have Siri respond with a rote answer of "I don't understand," they did an amazing job of anticipating some of the questions people would ask and crafted humorous and heartfelt responses.

It's that attention to detail that is a hallmark of Apple products, and why Siri has become so popular in the media. Other voice-control and device-navigation systems are available, but none are as seemingly human as Siri. Hopefully, you've stopped laughing enough to take away the following key points from this chapter:

- While tweeting and blogging aren't yet directly supported by Siri, workarounds let you use text messaging services and email to send your statements to the world.

- It's okay to be silly with Siri, one of the iPhone 4S's best show-case features. If using its built-in humor and whimsy are useful in demonstrating those features, why not go for it? There's nothing wrong in taking pride in your phone. Let Siri show-case itself and provide a little entertainment.

- Ask Siri about itself, and you'll be amazed and amused with its responses. In many respects, Siri is a reflection of the clever design team that created and is evolving this astounding software.

- Siri's connections to Wolfram Alpha provide it with a huge storehouse of pop-culture references and make it your go-to mediator for arguments dealing with trivia as well as math and science questions.

Dictation

The preceding chapters of this book have shown you how Siri works with your spoken voice to serve your needs and answer a lot of questions. Apple's intelligent assistant does much more than just answer questions and make jokes, and that's what this chapter is all about.

One of the key features of Siri is its ability to take dictation. That means that it can listen to your voice and translate your spoken words into text. Through dictation, you can reduce your usage of the tiny keyboard of the iPhone and leave the typing to Siri.

In this chapter, you learn how to get the most accurate responses from Siri through fun examples and practice phrases. Siri knows how to add punctuation if you tell it to do so, and you will find that it's remarkably good at taking notes or even writing short documents.

Siri has a good working relationship with other computers, so this chapter show you how to use third-party software on those computers and your iPhone to enable dictation. This extends Siri's excellent dictation capabilities to your personal computer, perfect for writing a novel without worrying about what too much typing does to your wrists and hands.

Enunciation Practice

Tongue-twisters provide a fantastic way for you to practice your Siri enunciation skills. Plus, they're a lot of fun to try to say right. Siri responds directly to each of the following twisty sentences (see Figure 7-1).

- How much wood would a woodchuck chuck if a woodchuck could chuck wood?
- How many pickled peppers did Peter Piper pick?
- What does she sell by the seashore?
- How many boards could the Mongols hoard if the Mongol hordes got bored?
- How many cans can a cannibal nibble if a cannibal can nibble cans?

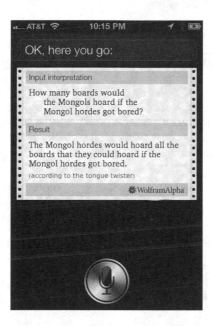

Figure 7-1
Train your Siri enunciation skills with these Wolfram Alpha-sourced tongue-twisters. It only took us about five dozen tries (We refused to cheat and use the utterance-editing features) to get this one right.

Dictation 101

You've seen how to access the Siri assistant by raising the phone to your ear and by pressing and holding the Home button. Another element of Siri appears on your iPhone keyboard outside the standard assistant interface: the dictation microphone. As Figure 7-2 shows, the microphone appears just to the left of the spacebar and to the right of the numeric toggle on the standard keyboard. Tapping this microphone offers another way to access Siri features.

NOTE

Make sure you match the Siri dictation to the language you are using. You may add keyboards via Settings, General, Keyboard, International Keyboards, Add New Keyboards. When you use multiple keyboards, select from these by tapping the globe icon. This icon appears only when you have enabled more than one language. In early Siri releases, Australian dictation users need to use the English (UK) keyboard.

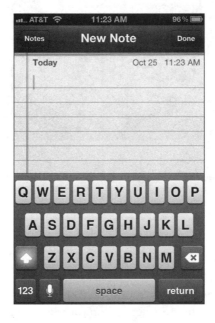

Figure 7-2
You can use Siri to dictate by tapping the microphone button found in the bottom-left of the System keyboard.

Hop into the Notes application. Create a new note, tap in it to expose the keyboard, and then tap the Siri microphone. When you do, a new Siri dictation screen appears (see Figure 7-3). This consists of a large keyboard-sized blue/gray background with the standard Siri microphone placed on it. This microphone works in the same way as the assistant interface, showing your voice levels as you speak.

Figure 7-3
Siri takes dictation.

Below the microphone is a large Done button. Tap this button when you have finished dictating and are ready to transfer what you have said into the selected text view or text field.

Read the following text. When finished, tap the Done button. In dictation mode, Siri does not use pause detection the way it does in assistant mode. Instead, it continues listening until you tap Done or until it runs out of listening space, at which time it automatically terminates your session.

> Alice was beginning to get very tired of sitting by her sister on the bank, and of having nothing to do: once or twice she had peeped into the book her sister was reading, but it had no pictures or conversations in it, "and what is the use of a book," thought Alice "without pictures or conversation?"

When you are done speaking, Siri goes into thinking mode, presenting a series of purple dots that flash until the interpretation is done. The interpreted text is then pasted into the note. Figure 7-4 shows what this might look like.

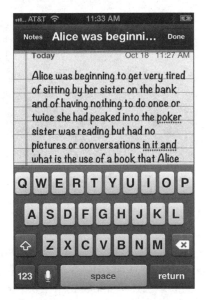

Figure 7-4
Siri tries its best to interpret the text you dictate into any text entry element on the iPhone. Notice the blue underline in this screenshot. A blue underline indicates multiple possible interpretations of your speech. Tap that word to bring up a bubble that lets you choose from possible words.

Notice there is no punctuation here. There are also misinterpretations, such as *poker* instead of *book her*. You can improve your Siri dictation in a number of ways to work around these issues.

Improving Your Dictation

The first rule of dictation is that you should always speak a little at a time. Although Siri can handle long, run-on sentences like the one you just read, it works better with shorter phrases. Second, enunciate. Remember how certain teachers always overemphasized each syllable? Pretend to be that teacher now, and reap the Siri rewards. Finally, supply punctuation, capitalization cues, and so forth to augment Siri's standard rules.

Here's an example for you to try. Try speaking the following as a series of dictation phrases. Speak slowly and clearly, including the extra items added to each bullet point:

- Alice was beginning to get very tired of sitting by her sister on the bank comma.
- And of having nothing to do colon.
- Once or twice she had peeped into the book her sister was reading comma.
- But it had no pictures or conversations in it comma.
- Quote cap and what is the use of a book comma quote.
- Thought cap Alice quote without pictures or conversation question mark quote.

This time, your results should look more like those shown in Figure 7-5. Here, there is punctuation, proper cases, and so forth. You can further improve your results by adding in information about sentence endings ("period" or "full stop"), new lines ("new line") to introduce a carriage return, and "new paragraph" to start entirely new paragraphs.

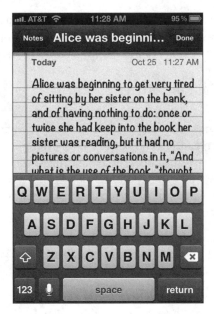

Figure 7-5
Dictating to Siri with grammar cues helps it include punctuation, capitalization, and more.

The following sections provide a rundown of the basic Siri dictation elements that you can incorporate into your dictation in addition to the ones shown in the preceding example.

Capitalization

Siri provides both immediate capitalization cues (for example, capitalize the next word) and modes (for example, capitalize until I say otherwise). When working with a mode in Siri, you specify what the mode is and when you are enabling and disabling it (via on and off). Table 7-1 details the Siri capitalization commands.

Remember as you use this that Siri defaults to capitalizing the start of new sentences and what it recognizes as proper nouns. You end a sentence by issuing a period, full stop, or by starting a new paragraph. In contrast, new lines do not start new sentences, and may not trigger capitalization of the next word spoken. You create line breaks by saying "new line" and paragraphs by saying "new paragraph."

Table 7-1—Capitalization

Command	Result
Capital/cap	Capitalize the next word or letter. (For example, my cat is named cap emerald becomes My cat is named Emerald. To type A.B.C., say Capital A dot, capital B dot, capital C dot.)
Caps on	Enable initial caps. (For example, oh boy becomes Oh Boy.)
Caps off	Disable initial caps.
All caps	Uppercase the next word. (For example, oh boy becomes OH boy.)
All caps on	Start caps lock mode. (For example, oh boy becomes OH BOY.)
All caps off	End caps lock mode.
No caps	Lowercase the next word. (For example, Erica becomes erica.)
No caps on	Start lowercase lock mode. (For example, Oh Boy becomes oh boy.)
No caps off	Ends lowercase lock mode.
Spacebar	Prevents a hyphen in a normally hyphenated word. (For example mother-in-law, so mother spacebar in spacebar law becomes mother in law instead.)
No space	Removes a natural space from between words. (For example, hello no space world becomes helloworld.)
No space on (and off)	Disables natural spaces between words. (For example, No space on this is my world no space off becomes thisismyworld. Make sure to pause after the initial *on* and before the ending *no*.)

To see Siri capitalization in action, try dictating the following. Make sure you leave a significant pause after any on/off command. We've included the hint pause in the dictation. Do not say "pause" there, just pause a bit before continuing the dictation. "Full stop" means end the sentence with a period.

Alice was beginning pause Caps on pause to get very tired of sitting by her sister on the bank pause Caps off pause, and of having nothing to do full stop. Pause All caps on pause Alice in Wonderland full stop. Pause All caps off pause The end full stop.

Figure 7-6 demonstrates what this dictation should look like when completed. Notice how the two modes (initial caps and all caps) are implemented in text.

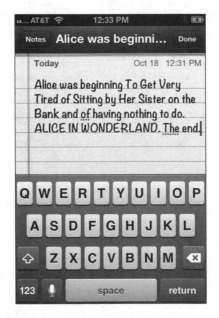

Figure 7-6
Siri capitalization commands are helped by pauses.

So what do you do when you need to use the word *cap* in a sentence, such as "I put a cap on my head"? You just say so. However, try saying, "When I write in all caps, it is lots of fun," and you will encounter difficulties.

Figure 7-7 shows how these two sentences appear after running through Siri. The first use is caught properly, but the second results in the awkward sentence "When I write in IT is lots of fun." (You can dictate "When I write in all caps comma, it is lots of fun" for the correct interpretation.)

Figure 7-7
Siri sometimes gets the context right, but sometimes not.

Punctuation

Siri understands most of the common punctuation names you throw at it. As Table 7-2 demonstrates, it responds to many of the items you find on the iPhone keyboard but not completely. For example, we have not been able to find a Siri entry for the bullet sign. There is room for growth in this arena.

Siri handles some items brilliantly, such as "full stop" to end sentences. It has trouble though where there are possible interpretation overlaps. For example, Siri misinterprets "single quote" requests as often or maybe more often than it succeeds in detecting them.

If you find punctuation items that we missed on this list (or any Siri dictation commands that fell through the cracks for any of this coverage), please contact us at info@sanddunetech.com and let us know. We did the best we could at documenting each element, but we did so through trial and error. We are sure there are valuable entries that we are missing here.

Table 7-2—Punctuation

Command	Result
New line	Insert a carriage return.
New paragraph	Begin a new paragraph.
Period (or full stop)	Add a period, finishing a sentence.
Dot	Add a period mid-sentence, without finishing the sentence. (For example, Erica dot sadun becomes Erica. sadun.)
Point	Add a period mid-number as a decimal point. (For example, Pi is three point one four.)
Question mark/ inverted question mark	Add a ? or a ¿.

Command	Result
Exclamation point/ inverted exclamation point	Add a ! or a ¡.
Ellipsis (or dot dot dot)	Add an ellipsis (. . .).
Comma/double-comma/ colon/semicolon	Add , or ,, or : or ;.
Minus sign/plus sign	Add − or +.
Quote (or quotation mark)	Add a standard double quote.
Quote… unquote	Surround the text with quotes. (For example, quote hello unquote becomes "hello.")
Single quote	Add '. (This works abysmally, so practice or you'll end up with lots of Hello single "World single" when you wanted to enter Hello 'world.')
Backquote/ampersand/asterisk	Add ` or & or *.
Open/close parenthesis	Add (or).
Open/close bracket	Add [or].
Open/close brace	Add { or }.
Dash (or em dash)	Add — (em dash), with spaces on either side. (For example Hello dash world produces Hello — world.)
Hyphen	Add – (en dash), without spaces on either side. (For example, Hello hyphen world produces Hello–world.)
Underscore/percent sign/at sign	Add _ or % or @.
Dollar sign/euro sign/cent sign/ yen sign/pound sterling sign	Add $/€/¢/¥/£
Section sign/registered sign/ copyright sign/trademark sign	Add §/®/©/™.
Greater than sign/less than sign	Add > / <.
Degree sign/caret/tilde/vertical bar	Add ° or ^ or ~ or |.
Pound sign (or number sign)	Add #.

NOTE

To date, we have been unable to find a "literal" escape mechanism to allow Siri to distinguish between the words for punctuation and their symbols other than spelling them out in lowercase without spaces.

Abbreviations

Siri offers a few simple abbreviations, as shown in Table 7-3. Siri does not have a lot of direct abbreviation support built in, and it failed on most of the academic abbreviations that we tested with. What you get are a few that are used very commonly in English.

Table 7-3—Abbreviations and Spaces

Command	Result
i e	Adds *i.e.* (with punctuation)
e g	Adds *e.g.*
Et cetera	Adds *etc*
p s	Adds *PS* (for example, PS I love you)
v s	Adds *VS* (for example, Sadun VS Sadun)

Smilies

Siri knows a few smilies, the text-based emoticons used in electronic communications. Table 7-4 details those that Siri supports.

Table 7-4—Smilies

Command	Result
Smiley/smiley face/smile face	:-)
Frowny/frowny face/frown face	:-(
Winky/winky face/wink face	;-)

Dictating Formatted Text

Siri understands many standard formatting options while you dictate. Here are examples of typical ways to use this built-in feature to simplify your dictation tasks.

Phone Numbers

Siri formats phone numbers to standard hyphenation. You do not need to say "hyphen" when entering those numbers. For example, you could say this:

> My phone number has changed from 3035551212 (full stop). It is now 5551919 (full stop). To order call 18005551313.

Siri produces hyphenated text for you because it recognizes the phone context for the numbers you fed it, as shown in Figure 7-8.

Addresses

Try dictating the following example to Siri:

> Sixteen hundred Pennsylvania Avenue Washington DC Two Oh Five Oh Oh.

Again, Siri correctly formats the results, producing a two-line address with proper ZIP code formatting, as shown in Figure 7-9.

Figure 7-8
Siri formats phone numbers for you with hyphens. You do not have to speak those hyphens out loud.

Figure 7-9
Siri automatically wraps addresses and properly formats ZIP codes.

Dates and Times

For basic dates, you do not need to speak any special formatting instructions. For example

> Thursday July Fourth Seventeen Seventy Six at Three P M

is converted to Thursday, July 4, 1776 at 3 p.m. But if you want to enter slash-formatted dates, you need to say the word *slash*. For example, you could say

> Ten slash one slash eleven at two thirty P M

to create the date 10/1/11 at 2.30 p.m.

Prices

Say the price as you normally would when talking to another person. For example

> It costs twenty dollars and thirty-two cents

produces "It costs $20.32." This is localized per region, so if you try to give pounds and pence or euros while localized to the United States, expect results like "It costs 3 1/2 pounds" or "It costs 15 euros" rather than £3.50 or €15.

URLs

Specify the w's (you say "dub") and the dots when dictating URLs. For example, you might say

> Dub dub dub dot apple dot com

to produce www.apple.com. Say "dub dub dub" to create the www prefix. It's cute, and it's fun to say.

Email Addresses

To dictate email addresses, say "at sign" instead of "at." You might say

> Her email address is Erica at sign Erica Sadun dot com

to produce "Her email address is erica@ericasadun.com." You can use underscores and dots in names; for example

> The email you're looking for is Erica underscore Sadun at sign Erica Sadun dot com

for erica_sadun@ericasadun.com. Once Siri recognizes an email address, it automatically removes extraneous spaces for a properly formatted address.

License Plates

Dictate license plates slowly, stating each number and letter. For example

> Colorado plate pause X pause Y pause W pause 3 6 7

correctly produces "Colorado plate XYW367." Practice shows that this feature works less well for all-letter plates and plates that don't follow common number/letter patterns.

 NOTE

Siri is not very accomplished when it comes to spelling out words. Do not expect to dictate letter-by-letter when working with Siri. That's not how the assistant has been designed.

Dictation Practice

Try entering the following letter into notes entirely by voice. You need not get every nuance correct (see Figure 7-10), but it should be a good exercise of your Siri dictation skills. Focus on trying to match the style wherever possible and learn where you encounter the greatest difficulties, and how to modulate your dictation skills to accommodate.

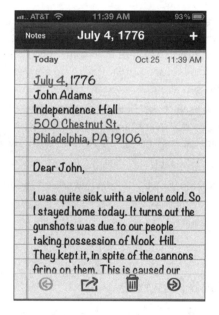

Figure 7-10
You'll be surprised how soon and how quickly you can dictate complex documents.

July 4, 1776

John Adams

Independence Hall

500 Chestnut Street

Philadelphia, PA 19106

Dear John,

I was quite sick with a violent cold. So I stayed home today. It turns out the gunshots was due to our people taking possession of Nook Hill. They kept it, in spite of the cannons firing on them. This has caused our Enemy to up and leave, or so I heard from a messenger just arrived from headquarters.

Some of the selectmen have been to the lines. They tell us that they have carried everything they could possibly take. What they could not, they burnt, they broke, or threw into the water.

This is, I believe, fact.

Please send me paper. I have only enough for one letter more. Or, you may call at 202-555-1414.

Yours, with full heart,

Abigail

Punctuation Practice

One of the questions that people keep asking us is how to spell out the word *comma* or *period*. In other words, how do you dictate the literal word rather than punctuation?

Fortunately, there is a solution for this. It's not an easy solution, but it can be done and be done cleanly in that you do not have to go back and remove extraneous punctuation the way you do if you try saying punctuation names twice (for example, comma comma or period period). To type out comma, you dictate "No caps on, no space on, C O M M A, no space off, no caps off."

This tells Siri to start a forced lowercase mode without spaces. You then spell out the word in question (comma, here). At the end, you return to normal dictation mode by disabling that mode.

Be aware that Siri looks for context. It can differentiate between "The Jurassic Period" and "The Jurassic." (see that period there?) during dictation, preferring the former because the word finishes a phrase.

Try dictating the following. These commands produce the sentence "I like to type comma and period every now and then," as shown in Figure 7-11. Make sure your include reasonable pauses as you move between lines and commands.

I like to type

no caps on, no space on,

C O M M A

no space off, no caps off

and

no caps on, no space on,

P E R I O D

no space off, no caps off

every now and then

Full stop

Figure 7-11
You can make Siri cleanly type the words comma and period, and other symbol names but these
don't come without significant effort.

Dictating to Your Computer

When enabled, Siri's dictation features appear in all apps that
support text, not just Notebook. Use the microphone button to
enter text by voice wherever you find a text field or text view. For
example, you can dictate search terms into Safari, speak names
into top scoring name achievement fields, and talk text into social
apps like Twitter.

Hooking dictation into third-party text entry opens the door to a
particularly handy trick. It lets you use Siri to enter text on your

home computer. Basically, you speak on your iPhone and text appears on the desktop.

It takes just a little work to get to that point. In the App Store, you can find dozens of apps whose job it is to transmit touches and keystrokes to computers. Any app that sends keystrokes can also transmit Siri dictation, letting you speak your text over to your computer. This provides a super-convenient solution for remote dictation.

Using VNC

Our preferred solution is built around *Virtual Network Computing* (VNC). This standard uses a special protocol called RFB to transmit key and mouse events from one computer to another. What makes it such a good solution for Siri dictation is that it's widely supported and that the data transmission is reliable. That is, the text you speak arrives in the order that you speak it.

With some third-party transmission solutions, when you say "hello world," the text may arrive as "elhlo world." That's because connection overhead may delay certain packets or third-party text enhancement apps may interfere with their injection. Many connection protocols are built in the time scale of a person tapping out keys on the iPhone. They just aren't robust enough to handle large chunks of text sent out as separate key press events. Those events overrun each other, the computer gets confused, and text arrives out of order. Our tests with VNC have shown it to provide the most reliable text transfer compared to other custom solutions.

VNC is built directly in to OS X. You enable it in the Sharing preferences panel (Sharing, Screen Sharing). On Linux, you enable Remote Desktop. On Windows, you install a VNC server like Real VNC (http://realvnc.com) or TightVNC (http://tightvnc.com).

On the iOS end of things, if you hunt through App Store, you can find a number of apps that let you enter text on your iPhone 4S and transmit it to your computer using VNC. We personally recommend Edivoia TouchPad ($4.99), which was the winner of my Remote Dictation Smackdown on TUAW.com.

Once you have installed it, you specify which server to connect to and enter your user credentials for your computer. From there, you can type text or move the mouse around by tapping on your iPhone screen. To use Siri, tap the microphone button on the keyboard and start dictation. TouchPad transmits that text directly to your computer, entering it into its frontmost application.

Other Apps

In addition to VNC-specific transmission, you can purchase apps like Mobile Mouse's Remote Dictate ($0.99) and RowMote Pro ($4.99). These require you to install a third-party server for your home computer, which is provided by the app developers.

In our tests, we found they suffered from transposition errors far more than VNC solutions. These apps were not designed for use with Siri Dictation. It's hard to ding them for not perfectly supporting a feature not in their original brief.

What's more, we have yet to find any app that properly allows for sentence capitalization and punctuation. That again is due to their design being centered on user key presses, not full dictation.

An opportunity exists here for developers who want to add "Siri dictation mode" to their existing apps or create a single-purpose app just for that reason. In that mode, you could imagine the app would provide more text style results, allowing toggles for such items as "Cap start of sentence," "Cap each word," and "Auto add end punctuation." We look forward to seeing that kind of functionality.

Summary

No speech-to-text dictation software is perfect, but Siri provides a steppingstone to the future of text entry. Understanding both the power and limitations of Siri's abilities is key to making use of dictation to take notes, send legible emails, and even create rough drafts of documents.

This chapter included the following information to maximize your use of Siri's dictation capabilities:

- Proper enunciation is key to making sure that Siri understands what you are saying before it converts your speech to text. Playing with complex tongue-twisters provides a great way to learn how to enunciate your words so Siri's dictation becomes more accurate.

- Don't be hesitant to dictate text to Siri, even though it will make some humorous (and frustrating) mistakes. Turn to the iOS keyboard and its interactive selection tools to patch things up after a long dictation session, and you will find that you're using Siri dictation much more often than you ever anticipated.

- You must tell Siri to add or remove capitalization and punctuation. This chapter provides all the phrases, knowhow, and techniques you need to dictate properly capitalized and punctuated text.

- Siri knows several common abbreviations and smilies. It is more than happy to enter them into your documents when you know the verbal shortcuts that get you there.

- Polish your skills for dictating formatted text, such as phone numbers, addresses, dates and times, prices, internet addresses, and email addresses. Siri knows how to format some of these items automatically, whereas others require you to phrase the text in a specific way.

- Extend Siri dictation beyond your iPhone. With a simple app purchase, you can speak text through your 4S to your computer, allowing you to dictate correspondence, reports, creative writing, and more using your iPhone natural language recognition system.

Index

FREE
Online Edition

Your purchase of **Talking to Siri™** includes access to a free online edition for 45 days through the Safari Books Online subscription service. Nearly every Que book is available online through Safari Books Online, along with thousands of books and videos from publishers such as Addison-Wesley Professional, Cisco Press, Exam Cram, IBM Press, O'Reilly Media, Prentice Hall, Sams, and VMware Press.

Safari Books Online is a digital library providing searchable, on-demand access to thousands of technology, digital media, and professional development books and videos from leading publishers. With one monthly or yearly subscription price, you get unlimited access to learning tools and information on topics including mobile app and software development, tips and tricks on using your favorite gadgets, networking, project management, graphic design, and much more.

Activate your FREE Online Edition at
informit.com/safarifree

STEP 1:   Enter the coupon code: TEMRUWA.

STEP 2:   New Safari users, complete the brief registration form.
Safari subscribers, just log in.

If you have difficulty registering on Safari or accessing the online edition,
please e-mail customer-service@safaribooksonline.com